JOHANNES GUTENBERG

Covering one of the most fascinating yet misunderstood periods in history, the MEDIEVAL LIVES series presents medieval people, concepts and events, drawing on political and social history, philosophy, material culture (art, architecture and archaeology) and the history of science. These books are global and wide-ranging in scope, encompassing both Western and non-Western subjects, and span the fifth to the fifteenth centuries, tracing significant developments from the collapse of the Roman Empire onwards.

SERIES EDITOR: Deirdre Jackson

Albertus Magnus and the World of Nature *Irven M. Resnick and Kenneth F. Kitchell Jr*

Alle Thyng Hath Tyme: Time and Medieval Life *Gillian Adler and Paul Strohm*

Andrey Rublev: The Artist and His World *Robin Milner-Gulland*

The Art of Anatomy in Medieval Europe *Taylor McCall*

The Art of Medieval Falconry *Yannis Hadjinicolaou*

Bede and the Theory of Everything *Michelle P. Brown*

Christine de Pizan: Life, Work, Legacy *Charlotte Cooper-Davis*

Francis of Assisi: His Life, Vision and Companions *Michael F. Cusato*

Frederick Barbarossa *G. A. Loud*

Geoffrey Chaucer: Unveiling the Merry Bard *Mary Flannery*

Johannes Gutenberg: A Biography in Books *Eric Marshall White*

Marco Polo and His World *Sharon Kinoshita*

Margery Kempe: A Mixed Life *Anthony Bale*

The Teutonic Knights: Rise and Fall of a Religious Corporation *Aleksander Pluskowski*

Thomas Becket and His World *Michael Staunton*

The Troubadours *Linda M. Paterson*

Johannes Gutenberg

A Biography in Books

ERIC MARSHALL WHITE

REAKTION BOOKS

For my mother

Published by Reaktion Books Ltd
Unit 32, Waterside
44–48 Wharf Road
London N1 7UX, UK
www.reaktionbooks.co.uk

First published 2025
Copyright © Eric Marshall White 2025

Printed and bound in India by Replika Press Pvt. Ltd

A catalogue record for this book is available from the British Library

ISBN 978 1 83639 039 8

CONTENTS

1 Bertel Thorvaldsen's bronze Gutenberg monument in Mainz,
engraving by Johann Poppel, after Ludwig Lange, c. 1855.

Foreword

The goal of writing *Johannes Gutenberg: A Biography in Books* was to provide an updated and contextualized account in English of the life, career, impact and legacy of Johannes Gutenberg, printer of Mainz. Gutenberg remains a problematic figure for historians in that he is often credited not just with originating the process of printing with moveable types for Europe, but, by extension, with a complex series of later developments that his work made possible, albeit which he never envisioned. Moreover, a widening divide exists between the historical Gutenberg, a man who left behind only a few dimly understood documents related to his actual activities, and the symbolic Gutenberg, the cultural hero immortalized in bronze in Mainz, who enjoys international familiarity as the pioneering 'prophet' of the vast media revolutions that continue into our days. Because the personality and thoughts of the man who died in 1468 may be lost to history, and centuries of local lore, competing claims and scholarly guesswork have confused, obscured or even inflated the essential facts underlying his work, the only way to get to know him may be through a closer look at the books and ephemera that he printed. They are the only possible reflections of his fifteenth-century concerns, ambitions, abilities and setbacks. A new assessment of his historical legacy that is sceptical of the stories that have always been told and is based squarely on the evidence of the surviving books attempts to get at what Gutenberg most likely did and did not do, and to clarify that while he exerted immense influence within fifteenth-century Europe (printing in Asia is another story), his ingenious work can only have influenced subsequent advances of liberty, science, thought and world literature indirectly. Whereas it does no one any good to exaggerate Gutenberg's historical agency, a clear retelling of what is known to be true, or is supported by the best evidence, will always be worthwhile. Truth needs no colour.

ONE

An Invention for Europe

I n the year 2000 numerous media outlets celebrated Johannes
Gutenberg (c. 1400–1468) as the 'Man of the Millennium'
on the basis of his unparalleled historical importance within
the realm of printing. Inevitably, arguments arose in favour
of alternative candidates from world history, many of whom
merited consideration on account of their lifesaving, peace-
keeping, humanitarian or rights-defending accomplishments,
while others were put forward because of the sheer magnitude
of their impact on human lives, or the loss thereof. Such debates
can never be settled. More consequential for our purposes is the
question of why, or whether, a fifteenth-century printer from
the German city of Mainz should remain a worthy subject of
widespread public and scholarly fascination some 560 years after
he last pressed ink to paper. The answer to this is not entirely
straightforward, as it is wrapped up in competing views of history, varying definitions of individual influence and changing
societal values over time.

It is absolutely safe to say that Gutenberg took the leading
role in the introduction of Europe's first method of moveable type
printing, which resulted in unprecedented quantities of virtually
identical high-quality books. Fortunately for Gutenberg's enduring fame, and for Europe, he lost his monopoly on typographic
printing in 1454, allowing others to introduce an unending
flow of ideas, manpower and capital to this dynamic new craft.

2 The Gutenberg Bible, 2 vols (Mainz, c. 1455).

By then, with the help of his first partners, Gutenberg had demonstrated that a lengthy text such as the Latin Bible could be multiplied for far wider distribution than had been imagined possible. Europe's first generation of typographic innovators developed a transferable technology that hundreds of printers across several kingdoms embraced within the first fifty years, thereby initiating a sustainable media revolution that opened previously unimaginable markets for profitable trade in books. In concert, Europe's fifteenth-century printers produced well in excess of 28,000 different editions – often in press runs of several hundred or even a few thousand copies – totalling perhaps 10 million books as well as countless single-sheet broadsides. Impressive as these numbers are, the real impact of Europe's first typographic editions was that for the first time, virtually identical copies of the same book could be consulted simultaneously by hundreds or even thousands of appreciative readers far and wide. In sum, the Western printing revolution up to the year 1500 had expanded and accelerated the dissemination of knowledge (broadly defined) so effectively that it becomes unthinkable that sixteenth-century Europe's relatively rapid and far-reaching developments in science, medicine, exploration, religious thought, governance, well-being, philosophy and literature could have taken shape without the agency of the printing press.

But this rather safe and limited summary of Gutenberg's impact on his contemporaries does not capture what led to his nomination as the 'Man of the Millennium'. The twenty-first century claims much more for Gutenberg. Schoolbooks assert that it is 'impossible to overstate the significance of Johannes Gutenberg's development of moveable metal type'.[1] Indeed, the prevailing view of his historical impact allows for extrapolations of cause and effect that extend well beyond his immediate sphere of activity and influence, implying that Gutenberg put his stamp not only on what he invented and accomplished, but on all of the future inventions of printing technology, the millions of books that resulted from them, and, by extension, the cumulative impact that those books have exerted worldwide ever since. On the premise that his prophetic vision provided the necessary illumination for all facets of technical advancement, Gutenberg's name is synonymous not only with printing across the centuries, but with progress and even modernity. Thus, when experts speak of the 'Gutenberg revolution' or about the 'post-Gutenberg' world, his name stands for the positive role of technology and mass media in the formation of the information superhighway and the present-day global village. Such an understanding of history leads to the conclusion that Europe's first printer truly was the most important man of the preceding thousand years.

On 7 April 1900, a full century before Gutenberg became the 'Man of the Millennium', Mark Twain took a somewhat different view when he composed a congratulatory letter regarding the opening of the Gutenberg Museum in Mainz. Its tenor was as insightful as it was unexpected:

In asking me to contribute a mite to the memorial to Gutenberg you give me pleasure and do me honor. The world concedes without hesitation or dispute that Gutenberg's invention is incomparably the mightiest event that has ever happened in profane history. It created a new and wonderful earth, and along with it a new hell. It has added new details, new developments and new marvels to both in every year during five centuries. It found Truth walking, and gave it a pair of wings; it found Falsehood trotting, and gave it two pair. It found Science hiding in corners and hunted; it has given it the freedom of the land, the seas and the skies, and made it the world's welcome quest. It found the arts and occupations few, it multiplies them every

year. It found the inventor shunned and despised, it has
made him great and given him the globe for his estate.
It found religion a master and an oppression, it has made
it man's friend and benefactor. It found War comparatively
cheap but inefficient, it has made it dear but competent.
It has set peoples free, and other peoples it has enslaved;
it is the father and protector of human liberty, and it has
made despotisms possible where they were not possible
before. Whatever the world is, today, good and bad
together, that is what Gutenberg's invention has made
it: for from that source it has all come. But he has our
homage; for what he said to the reproaching angel in
his dream has come true, and the evil wrought through
his mighty invention is immeasurably outbalanced by
the good it has brought to the race of men.[2]

Twain's words of wisdom captured something that the media
pundits of the turn of the subsequent millennium tended to
overlook: the downside that comes with the drastic and hasty
amplification of any human activity. Not forgetting the impact
of all the misinformation, fraud, tyranny and hate that already
had rolled off the presses, Twain showed a more focused and
nuanced understanding of Gutenberg's legacy. Still, he attributed all agency and its infinite outcomes to the inventor himself,
making him the prime mover of change, good and bad, on a
global and millennial scale. This was one great man's view of
another, heavily invested in primacy and achievement. Similarly,
but without a trace of Twain's sly scepticism, media outlets in
Y2K were anxious to trace the direct line that led from Gutenberg
to Google: just as his invention had democratized knowledge,
so the technological turn that he inspired had ushered in the
Internet Age. Today, however, perhaps inevitably after two
fraught decades of urgent social reckoning, the scepticism is

back. The often binary world of academic discourse has given rise to a popular viewpoint that not only questions traditional celebrations of Gutenberg, but dismisses his fame as some sort of fraud, perpetrated by the Western patriarchy as part of its long-standing conspiracy to entrench traditional notions of Western cultural superiority. There is admittedly more than a kernel of truth in this rhetoric. The Western patriarchy has found the unwitting prototypographer quite useful. But here we will be wise to differentiate clearly between fifteenth-century events and the subsequent writing and overwriting of that history. Younger generations with diverse viewpoints will subject the heroes of the Western tradition (and their biographers) to some healthy reconsideration. They may well ask what exactly was 'global' about fifteenth-century printing in Mainz. Which specific societal changes for the betterment of all did Gutenberg personally bring about? What was his actual role in the spread of literacy and education, the rise of democracy and the establishment of intellectual freedom? To what extent did he instigate or enact these beneficial changes himself – or has someone been left out of the narrative? These are legitimate questions that invite serious, well-researched answers. Ultimately, a thoroughly fact-checked, rethought, downsized and refocused vision of Gutenberg, one that does not overstate his impact or inflate his relevance around the world, will provide a path to a more balanced, global history of printing and its impact on human affairs.

Gutenberg died in February 1468. As far as book survivals can attest, up to that point a total of perhaps two hundred editions had been published in Europe, mainly in Mainz, most of which were not from his press. Other presses had popped up at least briefly in Mainz, Strasbourg, Bamberg, Vienna, Utrecht, Subiaco, Rome, Cologne, Eltville and a couple of places not remembered – but no printing had emerged yet from the great publishing centres of the near future, such as Venice, Paris, Lyon,

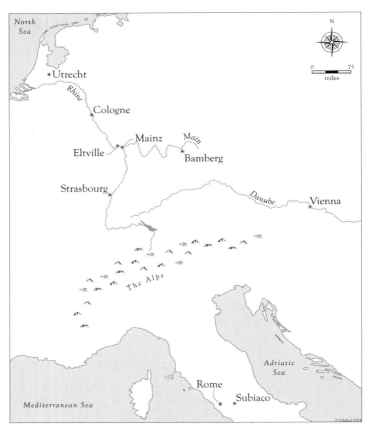

3 Europe's printing towns at the time of Gutenberg's death,
February 1468.

Milan, Augsburg, Nuremberg or Leipzig, much less anywhere
in such kingdoms as France, England and Spain or those of
Scandinavia or Eastern Europe. The overwhelming majority
of the printed books were Christian texts, focused on the Latin
scriptures, liturgy, papal decrees, theological writings of St
Augustine, St Thomas Aquinas and Jean Gerson, and calumnies
against Islam; among the secular works were a Latin dictionary
and various schoolbooks, German fables and allegories illustrated with woodcuts, and medical broadsides that prescribed

schedules for blood-letting. As for the Classics, there were some
key works by Cicero, but no Virgil, Livy, Pliny, Aristotle or anyone writing in Greek. The majority of the Classics were to appear
within the next few decades, as were the more useful works of
science, geography and history. Already by the year 1500, the
presses in Venice alone had outproduced those of Mainz more
than tenfold; meanwhile, many of Gutenberg's books already
had fallen out of use. Important though he was, Gutenberg lived
to 'see' less than 1 per cent of Europe's fifteenth-century typographic output, the great majority of which would come from
countries he never visited and printers he never met. It was only
during the centuries following Gutenberg's death that the en-
croachment of European influence overseas made it possible for
Europe's ever-evolving printing methods to extend their reach
to all corners of the world.

Before reconsidering Gutenberg's actual individual achievements, it is necessary to situate them properly within the worldwide history of printing. Gutenberg was born seven centuries
after important albeit nameless inventors in China initiated
the printing and reprinting of books by manually rubbing paper
onto carved woodblocks bearing ink; four centuries after
Chinese and later Tangut and Uyghur artisans printed from
moveable wooden or ceramic types; and several decades after
Korea's royal printers achieved impressive results with moveable cast-metal types, as exemplified by the *Jikji*, printed in 1377.
Closer to Europe, block-printed Arabic *ṭarsh* scrolls (illus. 4)
date from the tenth century, and given their widespread use by
the migratory *Ghuraba'* (Roma) culture, such amulets could have
been known in Germany in Gutenberg's time. Many nations
knew how to print pictures or decorative patterns from relief
blocks or engraved plates. Although the European inventor
of typography may well have been the first to arrange individual inked letters on a press, he was neither the first to print

textual multiples nor the first to cast moveable types.

It is fair to ask, as many have, whether Gutenberg was influenced by Asian printing. The search for Asian connections has proved to be an attractive but frustrating line of inquiry. Long-distance trade was welcomed in Mainz, where there was familiarity with silks, spices and perhaps other Asian goods. Over the centuries the Chinese papermaking craft had made its way to Europe, first along Muslim trade routes to Spain, then to Italy. However, we have no evidence of a 'type road', or records that anyone in Asia found reason to send printed books or specimens of printed currency all the way to fifteenth-century Germany; such things could not have carried commercial value where virtually no one was able to comprehend them (even Marco Polo famously neglected to mention Chinese printing). It would be one thing to communicate a need for nutmeg via traders over thousands of miles; getting coherent instruction in Chinese or Korean printing methods would be quite another matter. Similarly, seeing a stray *ṭarsh* amulet or a specimen of Chinese money does not lead one

4 Islamic *ṭarsh*, woodblock-printed scroll, Egypt?, 11th century?

to invent typography. But let us suppose for the moment that traders came to Mainz in 1450 with a copy of the *Guoyu*, recently printed in Korea with moveable metal types (illus. 5). What would Gutenberg have made of it? Could he have been attuned closely enough to the style of the characters to determine whether or not they were written by hand? Each page has only a handful of repeated characters; would he have noted that circumstance, and if so, would he have been able to conclude whether they were stamped individually in sequence or together, simultaneously? If he had correctly surmised the latter, could that have led him to back-engineer a method for mass-producing such characters and beautifully printed pages? For that matter, how would a solitary Korean book convey the crucial point that it was a multiple from a much more extensive edition of identical

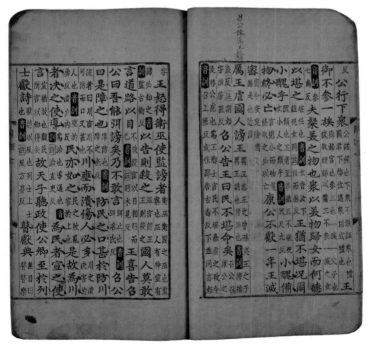

5 *Guoyu* (Korea, 1434), printed with moveable metal types.

copies, thereby inspiring someone to work out the problem of typographic multiplication? Even if Gutenberg somehow had worked out each facet of the book's nature, by simply looking at it he would have had very little on which to base an opinion regarding the faraway methods of type manufacture, composing the types neatly, inking them and impressing hundreds of copies.

It is not enough to wager that fifteenth-century Europeans were afforded forgotten glimpses of Asian printing. Importing the earlier printing technology would have required far more face-to-face exchange of specialized knowledge and practical experience than was possible. Although there was occasional diplomatic correspondence between the global extremities, such as that of 1289 between embassies of the Mongolian emperor Arghun and King Philip IV of France (each side writing in its own language), Gutenberg's contemporaries along the Rhine had difficulty getting reliable intelligence from as far away as Constantinople. Given that they still found manuscripts written in Greek essentially inaccessible, how then would they have communicated effectively with printers in the capital of the Ming dynasty? The unavoidable conclusion is that too much essential technical information would have been lost in translation along such extended trade routes. Meanwhile, Gutenberg himself is not known to have travelled for long periods at any point. Therefore, he is not to be credited with a forgotten ambassadorial role in the spread of East Asian methods of printing westward – a titanic feat of transcontinental synthesis that truly would have made him the 'Man of the Millennium'.

Woodblock printing flourished in China, Japan and Korea for several centuries, not as an inferior solution that was awaiting supersedure by moveable type printing, but as the preferred and most sustainable method of printing texts as well as images. But it was different in Europe, where woodcutting techniques for producing images thrived, while those for conveying texts withered. Simple woodcut devotional images emerged in Western Europe near the beginning of the fifteenth century and long remained popular. The late 1440s saw the development of hybrid books made with woodcut images and handwritten texts, of which the earliest known example is the *Exercitium super Pater Noster*, attributed to Hendrik van den Bogaert (1382–1469), prior of the Augustinian canons regular of Groenendael near Brussels, who wrote that he had conceived of the 'Exercise on the Lord's Prayer with pictures' in 1447. A more versatile and widespread innovation was the blockbook, in which both the texts and images were printed from a single carved wooden block per page. The most popular of the blockbook genres included the *Biblia pauperum*, a pictorial typology of Old and New Testament stories; the *Ars moriendi*, spiritual preparations for a Christian death; and the *Apocalypsis Sancti Johannis*, the otherworldly visions that St John described in the Book of Revelation. The earliest datable blockbook, a Netherlandish *Apocalypse* at the John Rylands Library in Manchester (illus. 6), has been dated by watermark evidence to circa 1452–4, by which time European moveable metal typography likewise was emerging from its development into production. By the 1470s, however, the blockbook medium was already on the wane as new genres of typographic books illustrated with woodcuts proved their marketability. Gutenberg appears never to have attempted to make an illustrated book, seeing that it was not worthwhile to compete in the niche market for blockbooks and utterly impossible to compete in the specialized market for manuscripts adorned with luxuriously illuminated images throughout.

Whereas both Asian and European woodblock techniques allowed for repeated printings of one particular text, Asian typecasting made purpose-built vocabularies of single-character words available for repeated printings of specific texts on demand.

6 *Apocalypse* blockbook (Netherlands, c. 1452–4).

By contrast, Europe's typographic method was based on the variable arrangement of individual types representing single letters of the alphabet. This made it possible to print an edition of any text in any language that used the Latin, Greek or Hebrew alphabets. The principal limitation of this more versatile system was that an edition, once completed, could not be expanded or reprinted on demand; the types had been dispersed and put away. Demand for more copies necessitated a new edition, that is, the manual composing of thousands upon thousands of moveable types into their proper order all over again. By 1460, as we will see, an even more complex printing technique arose in Mainz as a remedy for the downside of moveable types, but it soon was abandoned and forgotten.

Gutenberg's career as a printer may have lasted little more than a decade or so, but given the pioneering and therefore challenging nature of his work, he must be considered remarkably prolific. In addition to the magnificent Gutenberg Bible, the lengthy Latin dictionary called the *Catholicon* can be assigned to his shop, along with two slender theological quartos, several Latin schoolbooks, five ephemeral pamphlets, three broadsides and at least three different indulgence campaigns. It is not assumed that Gutenberg worked alone, or that he printed the two-volume Bible himself. Contemporary litigation shows that he borrowed substantial sums to cover the wages of several workmen before 1455, and that his costly 'work of the books' (*werck der bücher*) was conducted in partnership with a capitalist named Johann Fust, who by 1456 had ditched Gutenberg in order to take on a second major printing endeavour in partnership with the young calligrapher Peter Schoeffer, who married Fust's daughter and continued to print in Mainz for the remainder of the century. Gutenberg, meanwhile, found new investors and appears to have remained active as a printer, more or less independently, into his sixties. As his life drew to a close, he may have been somewhat famous; if not, he was about to become very much so.

Numerous fifteenth-century sources credited Gutenberg with the invention of printing. Their claims seem to be reliable not only on account of their quantity and consistency, but because they were broadcast without any evident fear of serious contradiction. The earliest of these appeared in 1468, two years after Fust's death and just three months after Gutenberg's. Peter Schoeffer's edition of the *Institutiones* of Emperor Justinian I, a code of civil law published with surrounding commentary in Mainz on 24 May 1468, concluded with an untranslatable Latin verse encomium of three divinely inspired craftsmen (here loosely paraphrased):

> Like Moses, whose tabernacle shone with the metalwork of Bezaleel, and Solomon, who ornamented his temple with bronzes cast by Hiram, He who is infinitely greater wished to renovate His church through the skill of two master sculptors born in Mainz, each named Johann, who gained honour as the founders of the art of stamping the characters of books. Along with them came Peter, who raced after them towards the monument they sought, but was the first actually to enter it; thus, it was to Peter that the Lord who alone bestows illumination and skill has granted even higher knowledge of engraving.[3]

This strange passage alludes to the Gospel according to John (20:3–6), in which St John the evangelist precedes the apostle St Peter in reaching Christ's empty tomb, only to see Peter be the first to enter. It was a showy and not very pious way of claiming that Gutenberg and Fust, despite their precedence in the field, had given way to the surpassing efforts of young Schoeffer, who indeed was the first to attain the finer typographic qualities of the small (and even smaller) types found in the present *Institutiones*. Interestingly, here Schoeffer allowed his late father-in-law to be represented as an equal partner in the 'sculpting' of the first types, which in effect Fust was, even if he had served more as the project's money manager than as a working artisan.

Schoeffer subsequently shared his own recollections of the rise of printing in Mainz with Johannes Tritheim, the learned abbot of the Benedictines in Würzburg, who in 1514 recorded them in his *Annales Hirsaugienses*.[4] Under a heading dated 1450, Tritheim recalled that nearly thirty years ago (that is, in the 1480s), Schoeffer had told him that Gutenberg was the inventor of the 'wonderful and previously unknown art of printing books'; at first (he claimed) Gutenberg had carved his letters from wood, and with Fust's help used these to print the *Catholicon* (a well-known Latin grammar and lexicon), but then with Schoeffer's assistance Gutenberg eventually perfected the casting of metal types, which the three men used to print a Bible that had required an expenditure of 4,000 florins before the completion of its third ten-leaf gathering. Tritheim's interpretation of Schoeffer's testimony is almost certainly somewhat garbled – there is as yet no other evidence for the evolution of Gutenberg's types from wood to metal, and the grammatical work that was printed first was probably the very brief schoolbook known as the 'Donatus' – but there seems to be no reason to doubt the overall narrative: Gutenberg was the inventor of the art of printing with metal types, Fust was the facilitator of their first publications and Schoeffer was the one who helped improve the typecasting so that a costly Bible could be printed.

A presumably unbiased attestation regarding the invention of printing came from the pen of Guillaume Fichet (1433–1478), professor of theology and librarian at the Sorbonne in Paris. In a letter that he wrote on New Year's Day 1471 to Robert Gaguin, a former pupil living at the nearby Couvent des Mathurins,

Fichet commended the benefits of the new art, which had been brought to Paris during the previous year:

> I speak of the restitution of humanistic studies, for which (as far as I can surmise) great light has been provided within recent memory by the new order of book-makers from Germany, who have poured forth everywhere (as from a Trojan Horse). For it is said that there, not far from the city of Mainz, one Johannes, surnamed Bonemontano [Latin for 'good mountain' – that is, Gutenberg], was the first of all men to conceive the art of printing, by which books are produced not with a reed, as the ancients did, or with a quill, as we do, but by means of letters made of brass, with speed, elegance, and beauty.[5]

Fichet was impressed not only by the usefulness of printing, but by how widely it had spread in a short time. If he were very well informed, he may have been able to list perhaps a dozen towns that had printing presses at that time. Commentators ever since have likewise been impressed by the speed of typography's spread across Europe: modern bibliographers know of some 240 towns that had at least one printing press by the end of the fifteenth century, while the leading centres had several competing presses. Was this expansion truly rapid? Compared to the spread of the plague, not at all; but after a slow first decade, it grew about as quickly as the taste for Gothic architecture spread beyond France. As far as it is known, printing never faced serious resistance in Europe: although the fifteenth-century Florentine bookseller Vespasiano da Bisticci once pretended that the magnificent library of Federico da Montefeltro, the learned Duke of Urbino, was so rich in manuscripts that 'had there been one printed volume it would have been ashamed in such company', in fact the duke eventually owned at least fifty printed books.[6]

A temporary sidestepping of Gutenberg's priority as 'inventor' was attempted already in 1471, when the humanist Omnibonus Leonicenus of Vicenza wrote in his preface to Quintilian's *Institutiones oratoriae* (Venice, 21 May 1471) that the publisher, the French émigré Nicolas Jenson, was 'a wonderful inventor of the art of making books'.[7] Although Omnibonus may have had in mind inventive improvements to the new art, this perhaps intentionally misleading slight of the printers in Mainz may have persuaded Jacobus Philippus de Bergamo to list Gutenberg and Fust as the first printers in his *Supplementum chronicarum* (Venice: Bernardinus Benalius, 23 August 1483), with Jenson listed third. Gutenberg continued to enjoy by far the most widely recognized claim to the invention, but he sometimes had company. The *Chronica summorum pontificum imperatorumque*, begun by Philippus de Barberiis (1426–1487) and expanded for publication in Rome by Johannes Philippus de Lignamine in 1474, provided a somewhat garbled account in its entry on the pontificate of Pius II (1458–64), under the year 1459:

> Jacobus [*sic*] surnamed Gutenberg, born of Strasbourg [*sic*],
> and a certain other whose surname was Fust, both experts
> in printing letters on parchment with metallic forms, were
> known to produce 300 sheets a day in the German city
> of Mainz. Likewise Johann, called Mentelin, a citizen of
> Strasbourg in the same province and expert in the same
> craft, is acknowledged to have printed just as many sheets
> per day.[8]

Several other accounts from 1474 to the end of the fifteenth century attributed the invention of printing to Gutenberg, and those that also mentioned Fust gave him no more than equal billing. These included the Meisterlied 'Vor langer frist' by Hans Folz (Nuremberg, c. 1480); the *Supplementum chronicarum* by

Jacobus Philippus de Bergamo (Venice, 1483); the *Chronica* by
Bossius Donatus (Milan, 1492); *De dictis factisque memorabilibus
collectanea*, compiled before 1494 by Baptista Fulgosus (first
printed in 1509); the *Lobgedichte* by Adam Werner and Johannes
Herbst (Heidelberg, 1494); and the *Orationes* by Adam Gelthus
and Jacob Wimpfeling (Mainz, 1499), compiled by Marsilius ab
Inghen. The earliest source to assign a specific *date* of origin for
Gutenberg's invention was the *Chronicon* of Eusebius, Bishop
of Caesarea (Venice: Erhard Ratdolt, 1483), a fourth-century
text translated from the Greek by St Jerome and updated by
several Italian scholars. Under the year 1457 one finds a notice
about Gutenberg's invention of printing, presumably added by
the printer Ratdolt, who hailed from Augsburg:

> Words cannot express how much the students of
> literature owe to the Germans. For in the year 1440
> Johann Gutenberg zum Jungen, knight of Mainz on the
> Rhine, with great skill invented a method of printing
> books. Now [in 1483] such books are distributed to
> almost all parts of the world; to such an extent that the
> whole of antiquity can be bought at a low price and read
> by succeeding generations in a multitude of volumes.[9]

The date '1440', two years prior to Ratdolt's birth, has no
known corroboration in eyewitness testimony and seems to
be about a decade too early. Abbot Tritheim indicated instead
a date of invention soon after his birth in 1452: 'For this art
called printing, invented at the Frankish metropolis of Mainz
in the time of my infancy, brings to light each day almost infinite volumes of works old and new.'[10] Was '1440' simply a typographic error or mistranscription? One of the continuators of
this *Chronicon*, Matteo Palmieri of Pisa, who was only seventeen
years old in 1440, likewise had mentioned the invention of

	❡ Anni mūdi	Anni Saluti	Anni Pont		❡ Impátoz Occidentis
p Librozr īpßio				❡ Quantū litterarū studiosi Germanis debeant	
				nullo satis dicēdi genere exprimi posset. Nāq;	
				a Joanne Gutenberg Zuitungē equiti Magū	
				tiē rbeni solerti igenio librox Imprimēdox	
	1440			ratio 1440.iuenta:boc tēpe i oēs fere orbis par	
				tes ppagat:q̄ omnis ātiquitas paruo erē cōpa	
				rata:posteriorib² infinitis voluminib² legitur.	

7 Early mention of Gutenberg's invention, in Eusebius of Caesarea, *Chronicon* (1483).

printing in his *De temporibus suis*, crediting 'Robertus Dusberch' of Mainz with printing more than three hundred books in the same time that it took scribes to write only a very few books with a pen.[11] However, Palmieri had situated the invention under the year 1449, which may have been the date intended in the printed *Chronicon*. As far as contemporary documents attest, the claim that printing was invented as early as 1440 was never promoted in fifteenth-century Mainz.

Gutenberg's inclusion in the Eusebian *Chronicon* is truly remarkable. This handy book functioned as a chronicle of the political and religious events that impacted Italian city states such as Florence, Milan, Venice, Naples and Rome. Therefore, the focus was squarely on Italy and the relevant deeds of emperors, princes, dukes, popes, bishops or future saints, with the occasional mention of comets, eclipses and plagues. Events in Germany were virtually ignored, and the individual achievements by those who were not political or ecclesiastical grandees were limited almost exlusively to those of Italian scholars whom the compilers knew and admired. A comparable *Chronicon* entry, albeit one with an Italian hero, celebrated the architect Filippo Brunelleschi's completion of the stupendous dome of Florence Cathedral in 1436; yet the praise reserved for Gutenberg's invention was lengthier and higher still.

Only one of the fifteenth-century publications that credited Gutenberg with the invention of printing identified a specific book that he printed. Indeed, the idea that European typography commenced in Mainz during the 1450s with a book that today is called the 'Gutenberg Bible' descends not from a statement within the Bible itself or any other strictly contemporary record. Rather, that memory was preserved only within Tritheim's recollection of Peter Schoeffer in the 1480s (which was not published until 1690) and in a somewhat later but nevertheless reliable source, a book known as *Die Cronica van der hilliger stat van Coellen*, printed in Cologne in 1499. This 'Chronicle of the Holy City of Cologne', compiled in Low German dialect by an anonymous Augustinian scholar, recounts the history of the city, including local events such as the foundations of churches or monasteries, as well as affairs of larger significance in relation to the papacy, the Holy Roman Empire and neighbouring kingdoms. The chronology pauses in the year 1450 for a special chapter

8 Early description of the Gutenberg Bible, in *Die Cronica van der hilliger stat van Coellen* (1499).

titled *Van der boychdrucker kunst*, that is, 'On the Art of Printing
Books' (illus. 8). It declares that this praiseworthy and useful
process was invented in Mainz and boasts that it came immediately thence to Cologne. The fact that Cologne's patriots were
eager to crown their city as second only to Mainz (whereas, in
truth, Strasbourg was probably second and Bamberg was third)
merely serves to verify that Mainz was indeed the first. The compiler of the Cologne *Cronica* was informed about all things
relating to printing by Ulrich Zel of Hanau (d. 1503), a former
cleric in Mainz who by 1466 had established the first press in
Cologne. The account of the wondrous invention begins:

> This revered art was first discovered in Germany, at Mainz
> on the Rhine; thus, it is a great honour for the German
> nation that such wise men were to be found there. It was
> in the year of our Lord 1440 and from that time until the
> year [14]50 that this art and all that pertained to it was
> investigated, and so it was in the year of our Lord written
> as 1450, which was a golden [jubilee] year, that printing
> began; the first book to be printed was the Bible in Latin,
> and it was printed with a large letterform, much like that
> with which they nowadays print Missals.[12]

According to the recollections of the venerable printer
Ulrich Zel in Cologne, typography was invented around 1450
in Mainz, where work soon began on the first printed book, a
Latin Bible featuring letters that were large and handsome like
those found in missals, the liturgical books for the celebration
of the Mass. The *Cronica* went on to mention, in cryptic terms,
the making of a *Donatus* in Holland – almost certainly a blockbook, carved from wood – that was a 'precursor' to the prevailing
method of printing, then paused briefly to refute Omnibonus'
clearly spurious claim of priority on behalf of Jenson in Venice,

and finally turned to the identity of the true inventor: 'But the first discoverer of printing was a burgher of Mainz who was born in Strasbourg, a squire [*joncker*] named Johann Gudenburgh.'[13]

Gutenberg was so well remembered as the inventor of the new art among contemporary printers and scholars that he should have been well placed to be remembered as such for all time. But Fortune's wheel turns in unpredictable ways. The sixteenth and seventeenth centuries would fail to remember Gutenberg and his achievement clearly, if at all, and his Bibles soon would be set aside and forgotten. Most of them were lost to the ages, and it was not until the eighteenth century that antiquarians would begin to look for the surviving specimens and treasure them again, not as useful books for reading the sacred scriptures, but as landmarks of great human invention. But the precipitous decline of Gutenberg's historical fortune – and his modern rehabilitation – is a story best told in our final chapter.

TWO

A Man Called Gutenberg

Although details of Gutenberg's life have long attracted the scrutiny of historians, the man is not someone whom his biographers, much less their readers, can get to know. There are no authentic letters, diaries, jottings, impressions or anecdotes. As far as surviving documents attest, no one in Gutenberg's time described him or his personality, and no one recorded what he was doing in any truly useful detail, much less what his intentions and ambitions were. All of the portraits that exist of him are entirely imaginary; most were influenced by an engraving in André Thévet's *Les vrais pourtraits et vies des hommes illustres* (The True Portraits and Lives of Illustrious Men), published in Paris in 1584 (illus. 9), which is virtually indistinguishable from the 'true portraits' of King Skanderbeg, Archimedes and the Venerable Bede in the same book. Gutenberg very probably did not defy contemporary German fashion by keeping a beard, and therefore he very probably bore little resemblance to the brooding Moses-like figure in a fur hat that so many later images have popularized. It would be better to cleanse those images from one's mind and imagine the inventor instead as someone just a bit older and perhaps a bit richer than the anonymous German subject of the mysterious Wolfegg Castle portrait (illus. 10). One of the earliest autonomous portraits in German art, this little drawing is decidedly *not* of Gutenberg, but compared to the spurious French engraving, it has the

9 Imaginary portrait of Gutenberg, in André Thévet, *Les vrais pourtraits et vies des hommes illustres* (1584).

advantage of being a century closer to Gutenberg's time, if not from his last years. Gutenberg and the man in the drawing walked in the same sunshine, spoke the same language and possibly knew people in common.

What does remain from Gutenberg himself, besides a haphazard and incomplete body of unsigned, mostly undated printed artefacts, is a small group of entirely faceless legal documents. These establish his whereabouts, offer dates and mention various transactions and activities, but they provide very little of the larger story concerning either his life or his most important invention. Moreover, his undeniable success was so mitigated by setbacks, complications and disagreements that no one at the time of his death in 1468 appears to have marked his passing with anything more than the most veiled reference to his achievements, and memorials of marble or bronze would not

10 Master of the Mornauer Portrait (attrib.), *An Unknown Man*, c. 1470, ink on paper.

arise until the nineteenth century. Therefore, the modern reteller of Gutenberg's story faces the difficult task of piecing together an account of his movements, decisions, actions, plans and relationships – entirely without recourse to his words or thoughts – on the basis of a woefully incomplete and randomly preserved body of evidence. Conflicting interpretations of this meagre evidence are inevitable, and there is the eternal challenge of separating historical facts from Romantic or patriotic fictions. A reasonably coherent biography emerges as long as one does not invent forgotten journeys, new controversies, doppelgängers or alternative scenarios out of nothing.

The main setting for the epochal events recounted here was the German city of Mainz – known since the twelfth century as

11 Imaginary view of Mainz, in Hartmann Schedel, *Liber chronicarum* (1493), also used to depict Naples, Bologna, Lyon and other cities.

Aurea Moguntia, 'Golden Mainz' – which Aeneas Silvius
Piccolomini, the humanist scholar, Imperial legate and future
pope (as Pius II), described in his *Germania* (c. 1457) as 'an
ancient city, the famed seat of the vanquished [Roman general]
Varus, adorned with magnificent temples and other buildings
private and public, which leaves nothing to criticize save the
narrowness of its streets'.[1] Mainz was not a large city, even in
the fifteenth century, numbering perhaps only 5,000 or 6,000
inhabitants, whereas Cologne and Strasbourg held several times
that number. But it was the most important ecclesiastical centre in the Holy Roman Empire, serving as the seat of a vast and
influential archdiocese that encompassed not only the bishoprics of Strasbourg, Worms and Speyer in the Rhineland, but
Würzburg in Franconia, Halberstadt, Hildesheim and Verden
in Saxony, Paderborn in Westphalia, Augsburg and Eichstätt
in Bavaria, and Constance and Chur in Switzerland. The archbishop of Mainz traditionally exerted immense religious and
temporal influence as the foremost prince-elector of the Holy
Roman Emperor, arch-chancellor and primate of Germany and
supreme papal legate north of the Alps. The archbishops who
presided over Mainz during Gutenberg's adulthood were Dietrich
Schenk von Erbach (1434–59), who appears to have looked
kindly upon the use of the press for religious texts; Diether von
Isenburg (1460–61), a reformer who enjoyed a loyal following
within the city; and Adolph II von Nassau (1461–75), who, with
the backing of Pope Pius II, used military force to usurp his
predecessor's chair. Given the immediate impact of printing on
Christian worship and thought, it is a near certainty that if printing had emerged from some other German town, the presiding
archbishop would have stepped in quickly to import it to Mainz,
lest it develop without benefit of his oversight.

The city of Mainz is nestled inside a great westward turn of
the mighty Rhine, which runs generally northwards from Lake

Constance through Basel and Strasbourg to Mainz, where a much smaller flow of water, the Main, breaks off to the northeast towards Frankfurt am Main. The Rhine itself then continues past Mainz and nearby Eltville to Rüdesheim and Bingen before turning north again towards Boppard and Koblenz, eventually passing through Cologne and the Netherlands on its trek down to the North Sea. Centrally located Mainz was extremely well connected to other towns in regard to trade, crafts, culture and religion. St Boniface, the 'apostle to the Germans', became the first archbishop of Mainz in the mid-eighth century. As his cathedral did not survive early fires, the grand Romanesque edifice that cast its shadow over Gutenberg's activities, the Dom St Martin, was a construction of the eleventh to the thirteenth centuries. Other churches in Mainz that Gutenberg knew well were St Christopher's parish church, where he was baptized; St Stephen's collegiate church, situated on the town's highest hill and known for the panoramic view provided by its bell tower; the church of the Barefooted Franciscans, near the centre of town; and the church of St Viktor, outside the city walls to the south, where in 1439 Gutenberg's second-cousin Jacob Gensfleisch was the schoolmaster, and where in 1457 Gutenberg himself was listed as a member of its small confraternity of lay-men benefactors. Gutenberg was also familiar with the monastery of the Carthusians of St Michael, situated on the riverfront, and the wealthy Benedictine abbey of St James, nestled within the ancient citadel to the south of the city. The latter two commu-nities are known to have purchased Gutenberg's early printed books.

Around the year 1400 Mainz offered its citizens opportu-nities for prosperity, but freedoms were limited by the self-protective policies of the craft guilds and the watchful authority of the Church, which ruled the secular law courts. The citizens' struggles for better representation in the workings of municipal

12 Mainz Cathedral (as rebuilt after the Second World War).

government were unending. On one side of the city council were
the annually elected representatives of the guilds, who had to
swear allegiance to the archbishop. On the other side were the
hereditary patrician counsellors, who enjoyed special privileges
granted by the Church as well as influence within its hierarchy.
These two sides were in constant political and economic conflict, as the guilds strove to limit the patrician monopolies in

the trade of cloth and precious metal along the Rhine, while the patricians thwarted the guilds' efforts to expand their rights and levy taxes on patrician trade. Although some patrician families saw immediate advantages in intermarriage with prosperous shopkeepers or their offspring, this led to exclusion from the higher echelons of the old social order, and so the divisions worsened. Ultimately, the guildsmen were doomed to focus precious little attention on the necessities of good government because they were consumed by the need to block the patricians at every turn. These political tensions, decreasing population and growing municipal debt (which the wealthy Church did little to alleviate) gradually caused Mainz to relinquish many of its former economic advantages; as the fifteenth century wore on, nearby Frankfurt am Main, a free Imperial city with a popular annual fair, became the true centre of trade within the region.

Gutenberg's date of birth is not documented, but the event must have occurred in Mainz or possibly nearby Eltville around the year 1400, a conveniently round number that falls between two outer termini, 1394 and 1406, which are entangled with the vital statistics of his parents and siblings. It is believed that Johann was baptized in the water of the large stone font that survives within the ruins of the St Christopher's parish church in Mainz. His father, Friele (Friedrich) Gensfleisch zum Laden, whose surname means 'goose-meat of the house of Laden', was the wealthy scion of one of Mainz's venerable patrician families. The coat of arms of the Gensfleisch clan (illus. 13) was visible throughout the Mainz region: on a field of red, a male figure strides towards the left, wearing a somewhat shabby cloak with a long pointed hood; a large sack is slung over his back, and he proffers a bowl in his right hand and carries a hefty walking stick in his left. Although the original meaning of the armorial is elusive, it most likely represents a wandering peddler, perhaps an allusion to the family's interest in long-distance trade. Friele

Gensfleisch registered as an adult citizen of Mainz in 1372 and assumed a hereditary position as a 'companion' of the mint that produced coinage for the archbishop. The future printer's father also served the city occasionally as its master of accounts, and had various business interests. Principal among these was most likely the cloth trade, the chief venture of his forebears and the staple industry of many of the Mainz patriciate. Some much later typographic preparations by his son included trial proofs

13 Armorial of the Gensfleisch clan, in *Lehnbuch des Pfalzgrafen Friedrich I* (1461).

printed on fragments from an account book concerning the garment cutters in Mainz during the years 1383 to 1392. Given the context, these accounts more likely belonged to Friele than to anyone else.

Friele's first wife, Grete Gelthus zur jungen Aben, brought into the world a daughter named Patze. In 1386 Friele married his second wife, Else (Elisabeth) Wirich (d. 1433), who provided the invisible labour that ensured the success of her husband's enterprises even after his death in 1419. She was the daughter of Werner Wirich (d. 1402), a wealthy spice merchant in Mainz, and Ennechen zum Fürstenburg, a Mainz patrician's daughter. Whereas Werner's father Nikolaus descended within the local patriciate, his mother Netta (Simonetta?) Ottini, whose name sounds Italian, did not. Her father Leo Ottini was a money-changer who managed 'Lombard loans' – accepting collateral much as pawnshops do – at nearby Bingen am Rhein, where there was another mint that served the archbishopric of Mainz. This fourteenth-century marriage of grandparents outside the closed circle of the Mainz patriciate would, in time, undermine the future printer's social and economic aspirations.

Friele and Else had three children: a daughter named Else, who married Claus Vitzthum the younger in 1414 and was still living in 1443; and two sons, Friele the younger (d. 1447), who married yet another Else, and Johann, the future printer (d. 1468). The earliest possible date of Johann's birth, 1394, has been calculated on the basis of a document of 1434 that quantified the annuities that his father had invested in the civic treasury for both of his sons in the proportion of seven to six, based on their ages. Since Friele the younger was born in 1387 at the earliest, and was at most 47 years old in 1434, Johann therefore could have been no more than 40 at that time; thus his date of birth was 1394 or later. Johann's latest possible birth date was in 1406, given the minimum age of fourteen that he must have attained by 1420, when a notarial document recorded that Friele the younger's little brother 'Henchen' ('Johnny') appeared without a legal guardian, thereby confirming his majority standing. However, the year 1406 seems very late, as his mother Else, born by 1370 and married in 1386, was by then pushing forty years or more. This minor but unsolvable conundrum is why historians simply place the inventor's birth 'circa 1400'.

Not long after his father's death in 1419, Johann came to be known by the name of a large stone house in Mainz, the Hof zum Gutenberg ('manor of the good mountain'). This house, owned by the patrician zum Jungen family at the time of his birth, became the property of his widowed mother around 1422, when she was referred to as Else zum Gutenberg. Documents do not record whether Johann pursued his education by means of tutors in his father's household at the Hof zum Laden, in a monastic or parish school in Mainz, or somewhere more distant. These were not to be idyllic years. In August 1411, when the guildsmen of Mainz violently protested the patricians' election of a conservative mayor who was determined to maintain their costly privileges, the patrician members were expelled from the city council, and Friele the elder was one of 117 heads of households who decamped (possibly quite willingly) from the city with his family. He presumably took them to nearby Eltville, where Else had inherited a house from her patrician side. Further civic tensions caused the family to flee again in January 1413, and waves of unrest erupted over the next few years. It is possible that young Johann remained in Eltville throughout this period to continue his education. In summer 1418 and winter 1419–20, just when Johann was presumably the right age to attend university, a certain 'Johannes de Altavilla' (of Eltville) matriculated at the University of Erfurt, 225 kilometres (140 mi.) northeast of Mainz. Although this fellow bore Germany's most common Christian name for boys, the suggestion that he was the young

Johann Gutenberg, who had not yet taken that surname, is bolstered by the fact that the future printer's cousins Frilo and Rulemand zu der Laden had matriculated at Erfurt in 1417, and his future business associate and executor Dr Conrad Humery was enrolled there in 1421. A university education can be assumed for Gutenberg, a last-born male offspring who pulled together several ingenious inventions, was capable of impressive practical and mechanical calculations and was well acquainted with Latin, its grammar and its written conventions. Clearly, Gutenberg's privileged status gave him the education, security and freedom to follow his own path in life.

Although the first three decades of Gutenberg's life are virtually undocumented, on 28 March 1430 he was listed among several expatriated patricians who were eligible to return to Mainz, a gesture of compromise with the civic government that was brokered by the archbishop after two years of heated political unrest. But Gutenberg may have decided that a return to Mainz was not worth the risk. Although he may have inherited his namesake property, the Hof zum Gutenberg, upon his mother's death in 1433, he did not live there for long; by 1444 the property was owned by Otto of Pfalz-Mosbach, Count Palatine. Indeed, from March 1434 until March 1444, Gutenberg was living not in Mainz, but in Strasbourg, a short journey up the Rhine. There, residing in the parish of St Arbogast just outside the city walls, he made a habit of falling into quarrels and litigation, as witnessed by the notarized letter of 14 March 1434 in which he agreed to release Nikolaus von Wörrstadt, the councilman and municipal clerk of Mainz, who had been arrested in Strasbourg at Gutenberg's request for failing to deliver 310 florins of overdue interest on his annuity. Granted, nonpayment of 310 florins (the cost of a handsome mansion) would have given anyone ample reason for concern, but the arrest of the leading guildmember of the Mainz council must have been seen as an outrageous tactic back in his hometown. Then in 1436 Gutenberg was named in an unsuccessful breach-of-promise suit brought by a patrician lady of Strasbourg named Ennelin zu der Iserin Thüre, and again in a successful defamation suit brought by the local shoemaker Claus Schotten, who, coming to Ennelin's defence, had said something that provoked Gutenberg to malign him as a liar and worse.

While it may be granted that the randomly surviving documents from this period often skew towards litigation and a need for societal guardrails, these three episodes nevertheless do not paint a pretty picture of Gutenberg's character. Another lawsuit having to do with contracts and secret enterprises would follow in 1439, while various other documents show that he was both a borrower and a guarantor of various loans in Strasbourg during the early 1440s, including one for 80 *pfund* from the Chapter of St Thomas in 1442 on which he and a certain Martin Brechter paid interest until 1458. In January 1444 Gutenberg was listed along with Andreas Heilman among the guild affiliates who registered for military service, and shortly thereafter, claiming to have less than 800 florins to his name, but more than 400 – still a comfortable fortune for a bachelor – he was obliged to contribute only one-half of a horse (that is, half of its price) to Strasbourg's defence fund. This tax was necessitated by the looming threat of the French mercenaries hired by the Dauphin Louis, known as the Armagnacs, who were plundering the Alsatian countryside. Following another four-year period in which nothing is known of Gutenberg's activities or even his location, he was mentioned in Mainz again from 17 October 1448, and he seems to have remained there, perhaps at the Hof zum Jungen, until at least 1457. Although the absence of relevant documents thereafter cannot imply anything about an absence from Mainz, it is virtually certain that he fled from the city (possibly to nearby Eltville) during the violence brought by the Archbishops' War in 1462. Finally, in January 1465 he was in Mainz when he received a generous pension as a reward for his faithful service to Adolph II, who won the archbishop's seat in 1461. Although Gutenberg was often involved in litigation concerning loans, he was never bankrupt or destitute. He died in Mainz shortly before 26 February 1468, when a local investor in a printing venture filed paperwork regarding his estate.

Gutenberg is often described as a goldsmith and as the son of an official of the mint in Mainz. Indeed, training in the mint and goldsmithery might seem to offer the perfect backstory for Gutenberg's singular role in the development of printing with cast-metal types. However, whereas Friele was at times concerned with the administration of the archiepiscopal mint, and Gutenberg himself often rubbed shoulders with goldsmiths, the professional associations alleged for both Gutenberg and his father have been overstated, oversimplified and misunderstood. Friele the elder's only association with a metallurgical craft was within the society of secular benefactors for the mint. His hereditary role as a 'companion' – supervisory and fiduciary, if not purely honorific – would have been more concerned with overseeing the treasury of precious metals than with the methods of the craft. No practical coin-minting experience was required of him. Nor would a patrician be allowed to master a craft controlled by a guild, such as that of the goldsmiths, whose members remained constant opponents of the patricians throughout the city's economic and political disputes.

Friele's son had no known connection to the mint, either in Mainz or elsewhere. Although he had patrician grandparents on three sides, which gave him entrée into most aspects of business and society in Mainz, the merchant-class lineage of his grandmother Netta disqualified him from assuming his father's hereditary place among the companions of the mint. Ironically, the mint was the one elite organization in Mainz that the future

inventor of printing could *not* join. Moreover, there is no evidence that Gutenberg attempted to descend the social ladder
to enter into apprenticeship or seek membership in the craft
guilds. Nor would the guilds have accepted him. In the period
1436–9, during which Gutenberg paid taxes on a large quantity
of wine stored in Strasbourg, he was designated expressly as a
resident alien who was not a member of a guild. In January 1444,
when Gutenberg and his business associate Andreas Heilman
registered for Strasbourg's military draft, they were listed as 'affiliates' of the master goldsmiths. Gutenberg's lack of guildmember
status was expressly stated, and yet his status as an affiliate shows
that *something* he was doing was thought to fall within or near
the jurisdiction of the guild of goldsmiths. Indeed, the fact that
he resided in the St Arbogast district (outside the city walls)
meant that he could fire up a forge, adjacent to his home or not
far away, something that only the goldsmiths were allowed to
do within the city itself. The document of 1444 should be seen
not as Gutenberg pushing for inclusion within the goldsmiths'
guild, but rather as guild administrators attempting to assert
their authority over his otherwise unsupervised activities. As far
as fifteenth-century documents attest, Gutenberg never prac-
tised as a goldsmith, and rules were in place to prevent him
from doing so; if any of the projects he conceived of involved
working with metals, then qualified craftsmen had to be the
ones paid to do that work. Europe's inventor of cast-metal moveable types simply may have directed others to undertake all
the furnace, foundry and casting work on his behalf, so that he
never personally worked with anything hotter than a bowl of
soup. Goldsmithery does not explain Gutenberg: the craft had
existed for millennia, yet none of Europe's goldsmiths thought
to invent typography.

What about Friele the elder's admittedly loose association
with the mint in Mainz? If this familiarity did entice his son to

take an interest in the practical matter of making coins, then what would the young inventor-to-be have learned as he watched the men work? Numerous coins such as the *gulden* (gold florin) and the silver *groschen* and *pfennig* produced for Johann II von Nassau, Archbishop of Mainz, survive from the period 1397 to 1419, precisely when Friele could have introduced his son to the daily workings of the mint. There, young Gutenberg could have seen the preparation of the iron pile, or anvil die, which was engraved with a circular relief image of the seated archbishop or a patron saint (for the obverse), and the cylindrical iron trussell, or hammer die, engraved with the heraldic arms of Mainz (for the reverse); and he could have watched as the circular gold or silver planchets (discs) of various weights were placed between the two dies, aligned by means of a surrounding collar, so that the trussell could be struck hard from above by a hammer, thereby embossing both sides of the coin simultaneously.

The striking of coins by the thousands involved neither a screw-press, as in printing, nor the fine casting of molten metal alloys in moulds, as in the production of printing types. Nor would a maker of printing types work with gold or silver, or employ the subtractive engraving technique that produced the recessed images in the iron dies for minting coins. Indeed, it is fair to ask, was there truly a meaningful connection between the mint and the type foundry? Medieval Europe counted thousands of people who worked in mints, but again, none of them went ahead and invented typography. In this regard, Gutenberg was the teacher, not the pupil. According to the earliest document that credits Gutenberg with the 'invention of printing' (long lost, but known from presumably reliable copies), on 4 October 1458 Charles VII of France dispatched Nicolas Jenson, master of the royal mint in Tours, to Germany to learn the art of printing from a nobleman in Mainz named 'Guthemberg'.[2] The French authorities evidently presumed that a master of their mint would be the most qualified person to comprehend Gutenberg's new method and bring it home. Twelve years later Jenson emerged as one of the greatest of all early printers – not in France, but in Venice. But Jenson was unusual among fifteenth-century printers for having earned his pedigree in the mint, and his trip to Mainz was necessary in the first place precisely because the making of types required knowledge and skills that even the master of the mint did *not* have. Seeking to print books with metal letters, the masters of the mints and the trained goldsmiths of the world were lost without Gutenberg, a man who was neither a goldsmith nor an affiliate of the mint, but an inventor of something new and mysterious to them.

Gutenberg's business-related litigation of 1439, in Strasbourg, is especially interesting because it mentions a manufacturing process. The Strasbourg documents, destroyed during the Prussian bombardment of 1870, revealed that Gutenberg was at work in the Alsatian city by 1438, contracting to teach Andreas Dritzehn the art of *stein bollieren*, that is, polishing stones. Thus Gutenberg's earliest known area of technical expertise pertained neither to the numismatic arts nor to goldsmithery. In that same year he entered into another partnership with a Strasbourg investor named Hans Riffe in which he retained a two-thirds share of a venture seeking to profit from his secret process for producing *spiegel* (mirrors) for pilgrims to Aachen Cathedral.[3] Earlier investigators into Gutenberg's past, naturally thinking in terms of printing, interpreted these 'mirrors' as printed copies of the Latin *Speculum humanae salvationis* (Mirror of Human Salvation), which indeed was one of the first devotional books to appear in print, albeit decades later. In fact, however, in 1438 Gutenberg was manufacturing not books for pilgrims to Aachen, but actual mirrors.

Of course, the traditional art of making mirrors was ancient, and it was hardly a secret. But Gutenberg and his investors must

have regarded his method, or the mirrors themselves, as special.
They were specifically intended for pilgrims wishing to travel
to Aachen in 1439 to witness, for the first time in seven years,
the public display of sacred relics from a tower high above the
Palatine Chapel. These relics, famous throughout Christendom,
had been presented to Charlemagne by the Patriarch of Jerusalem
in the year 799: the gown worn by the Virgin Mary on the night
of the Nativity of Christ; the infant Christ's swaddling cloth;
the Crucified Christ's bloodstained loincloth; and the cloth used
to wrap the severed head of St John the Baptist, the first witness
to Christ's divinity. Tens of thousands of believers from across
Europe made this pilgrimage, and they liked to have souvenirs
of their trip and reminders of the spiritual benefits they had

14 Aachen pilgrim's badge, Germany, late 14th century, cast lead-tin.

gained. Pilgrims' badges served these purposes well (illus. 14), signifying which destination had been visited and certifying that the act of pilgrimage had earned heavenly grace. While it may have been difficult to argue that mere metal badges were themselves true mechanisms of grace, badges with mirrors attached offered a special benefit. According to medieval tradition, mirrors held up in the presence of sacred relics were able to not only reflect the holy images, but 'capture' them. Mirrors infused with this power are seen in a 1487 woodcut of bishops displaying the regalia of the Holy Roman Emperor at Nuremberg (illus. 15). The theology (so to speak) underlying this pious hoax was that the salvific and healing powers that emanated from the sacred relics could be retained within the mirror, thereby converting the mirror into a kind of portable reliquary that could be transported home to be present in times of need.

There is no hint in the Strasbourg documents that Gutenberg's production of pilgrims' mirrors was in any sense authorized by the Church or was intended to benefit Aachen Cathedral. Instead, it appears to have been an opportunity for Gutenberg and his partners to capitalize on religious fervour in order to enrich themselves. As it happened, little about the mirror enterprise proceeded according to plan. Soon, two more local men, Andreas Dritzehn the stone polisher and Andreas Heilman (another 'affiliate' of the goldsmiths in 1444), gained insight into Gutenberg's secret plan and induced him to permit them to invest heavily in his project. Now Gutenberg owned one-half of the venture, Riffe one-quarter, and Dritzehn and Heilman one-eighth, each share costing 80 florins. Soon, however, it was learned that an outbreak of the plague at Aachen necessitated the postponement of the showing of the relics until 1440. With no immediate market for their many mirrors, the disappointed investors convinced Gutenberg to enter into a broader five-year venture that they would support with even larger investments,

15 Pilgrims with mirrors, woodcut in *Heiltum zu Nürnberg* (1487).

during which he would instruct them in all of the 'enterprises and arts' (*afentur und kunst*) that he might undertake, keeping nothing secret from them. Clearly, rich men in Strasbourg were impressed by the profit potential of Gutenberg's projects. However, fate dealt an even greater blow: at Christmas 1438 the deeply invested Andreas Dritzehn suddenly fell ill, perhaps of the coming plague, and died. His brothers Jörg and Claus Dritzehn repeatedly asked to take his place as partners in the five-year venture, but by contractual agreement the interests of the deceased reverted to Gutenberg, Riffe and Heilman. Not wishing to divide his business unnecessarily, Gutenberg refused, and so the Dritzehns sued.

Numerous witnesses were called, and many statements regarding Andreas Dritzehn, the partnership, shares, payments and purchases of lead ensued. But for historians interested in Gutenberg's activities, the bombshell revelation was the repeated testimony that after the death of Dritzehn, who had called himself a 'mirror-maker', Gutenberg's principal concern was that people visiting the house of the deceased might see the 'four pieces lying in the press'. What were these 'four pieces', and what was their purpose? The testimony was intentionally vague, and indeed Gutenberg may have winced even as the words 'four pieces lying in the press' were uttered. Upon the news of Dritzehn's death, he had asked Conrad Saspach, the trusted maker of the *presse*, to go and loosen the two hand-screws to allow the four pieces to fall apart, lest someone arrive at an understanding of their purpose. He made no similar provision for the press itself, which may indicate that it was a fairly generic and not particularly essential part of his operation. However, all too predictably, when Saspach arrived at Dritzehn's house, the crucial 'four pieces' suddenly were nowhere to be found. Now who could have made off with them? Frustrated and full of regret, Gutenberg asked his colleagues to make sure that any 'forms' (not necessarily mirrors) left on the press would be melted down, presumably to hide their purpose and to save the metal for another day.

The verdict in the lawsuit, read on 12 December 1439, ruled in favour of Gutenberg. He had argued convincingly that Andreas Dritzehn initially paid him for instruction on how to polish stones, and that being done, Dritzehn's heirs were owed nothing; further, the new contract for the extended venture clearly had stipulated that if any partner died within the first five years, then the investment would revert to the partnership with only 100 florins returned to his heirs. In fact, the deceased partner had not paid up the entire deposit. Therefore, in the eyes of the law, Dritzehn's brothers had no claim to Gutenberg's secret enterprise. But they did not go away empty-handed. Amazingly, items that had gone missing from Andreas's house in December 1438 rematerialized in 1446, now in the possession of Jörg Dritzehn. These included the press and the *snytzel gezug*, the cutting tools. According to the civic document of 1446, Jörg was being sued by his brother Claus, who in turn had sued him for not dividing other valuable property of the deceased evenly. These documents make no mention of the rightful owners, Gutenberg or his former partners. It seems that the Aachen enterprise was by then a distant memory and a lost hope. Indeed, it is possible that by 1446 Gutenberg was no longer residing in Strasbourg.

Did Gutenberg's ill-starred partnership successfully wait out the postponement of the pilgrimage to Aachen and actually sell their mirrored badges in 1440? Many metal badges with mirrors for the Aachen pilgrimage are known from the fourteenth century onwards. It is worth considering what they were and what they were not, and how they may have related to the metallic arts that Gutenberg would practise in the 1450s. Many of the earlier badges were made of cast metal. They consisted of the mirror itself surrounded by a Gothic framework supporting simple relief images of the Virgin and Child, Charlemagne, the

Bishop of Aachen and Mary's displayed gown. The manufacture of badges required three different skills: (1) the engraving of the badge design into both halves of a shallow soapstone mould; (2) the casting process, that is, pouring a molten pewter lead-tin alloy into the jet of the closed mould; and (3) the polishing and setting of the mirror in the badge. As the melting point was low and the cooling time was quick, the casting operation only took about a minute and could be repeated all day. The only parts that required real expertise, adding time and expense, were the production of the casting mould and the polishing of the mirror. Such badges cannot have been the subject of secret partnerships and desperate litigation.

As the fifteenth century progressed, pilgrim badges began to be stamped instead of cast. They were less like open-work jewellery and more like thin metallic wafers, embossed with a sacred image and provided with eyelets so that they could be easily sewn to the pilgrim's clothing. In this process (1) a metal die was engraved with the proper contours and recessed image required for the badge; (2) a small sheet of thin lead-tin alloy was placed in the stamping mechanism; and (3) either hammering or mechanical leverage was used to stamp the design into the cold metal sheet so that it was raised in relief. Sequential stamping with two dies, first to establish the shape of the badge and then its internal design, was also possible.

What was the nature of Gutenberg's mirror-making process, and why, unlike all others, did he have to keep his work so secret? Andreas Dritzehn was trained in polishing stones and later identified himself as a mirror-maker. Witnesses in the lawsuit of 1439 mentioned quantities of lead and 'forms' that could be melted down – not as part of their production but as a means of reclaiming leftover metal – as well as Gutenberg's concern that 'four pieces', screwed together in a *presse* in Dritzehn's home, might be seen and understood, thereby risking the partnership's ability to monopolize its market. Eventually the Dritzehn brothers confiscated the *snytzel gezug*, tools for cutting. This is all as cryptic as could be, but as none of the witnesses mentioned a furnace, moulds or casting, it sounds much more like a hinged mechanism for cold-stamping metal forms in an engraved die than a method for melting and casting them. The most intriguing testimony of all came from a goldsmith named Hans Dünne, apparently hired to perform tasks that Gutenberg could not. Dünne revealed that three years earlier (in 1436) he had earned about 100 florins just for his work pertaining to *trücken*. Originally this German gerund pertained to 'pressing' generally, or in certain contexts, 'forcing'. In 1428, however, the noun *Bilddrucker* was used in Mainz to identify the profession of a 'picture-printer' named Peter Schwarz, and by 1462 the term *gedrucket* definitely had been adapted to mean 'printed' by typographic means.

Later historians of printing, naturally more interested in Gutenberg's mysterious enterprises and arts than his mirrors, assumed that the five-year venture that began in 1438 continued out of the *trücken* that Hans Dünne undertook in 1436, and they concluded that the *presse* made by Saspach was a printing press. Further, these historians were eager to reconstruct Gutenberg's 'four pieces' as the mould for casting printing types – the ingenious apparatus that Joseph Moxon would illustrate in his *Mechanick Exercises of the Whole Art of Printing* in 1683 – which consisted of a hand-held metal sandwich that housed a removeable casting matrix for each letter while providing access for the molten metal to pour through an adjustable shaft. In short, the consensus of historians was that Gutenberg was already preparing to print quantities of books in ink on paper with moveable types at Strasbourg during the late 1430s. The Aachen mirror venture, a diversion of time and funds away from this alleged book project, was explained as Gutenberg's effort to raise capital for the longer drive to the main goal.

There are major problems both with this interpretation and with this chronology. What *trücken* meant to Hans Dünne in 1439 is by no means clear, and it must be emphasized that no unambiguous evidence of typographic printing, physical or documentary, exists from the 1430s or the 1440s, either in Strasbourg or anywhere else in Europe. The testimony never mentions the making of books, the casting of metal types or quantities of paper and ink, all of which may be very good evidence that no one had any such things on their minds. Although we must be cognizant of their desire for secrecy, and open to the possibility of false starts, loose connections and incremental progress, it remains difficult to see continuity between Gutenberg's projects of the 1430s and those of the 1450s, especially if his badges for pilgrims were stamped and not cast, while his printing types would be cast but not stamped. Moreover, the excitement Gutenberg had caused among investors in 1438 appears to have faded quickly. His five-year enterprise lapsed in 1443 and evidently was not considered worth renewing. After March 1444 the documentation relating to Gutenberg goes silent for four years, during which he eventually ceased his activities in Strasbourg and moved back to Mainz – a city now governed by the guilds, albeit under the superintendency of the Church. There, on 6 October 1448, he borrowed 150 florins (for unknown purposes) through one of his kinsmen, Arnold Gelthus, in a transaction witnessed by the master of the cathedral school, Volpert von Ders, who affixed his green wax seal. Although Volpert may well have been on the lookout for affordable schoolbooks for his pupils, there is nothing in this loan agreement that suggests such books were ready to come off of a printing press any time soon. Ultimately, none of Gutenberg's work during the 1430s can be shown to be connected to the production of books. For Europe, at least, finding a mechanical means of multiplying texts would remain a problem for a future decade.

A final thought on the Aachen pilgrims' mirrors: we know that thousands of them were manufactured to different designs, evidently by multiple vendors, to be sold quite cheaply during every pilgrimage year; however, it must be admitted that, barring miracles, they did not really work as intended (or as claimed, as the case may be). Is it then not possible, or indeed probable, that Gutenberg's mirrors offered something novel that would make them seem truly efficacious, and therefore desirable, for pilgrims? Was there some secret feature that made them, unlike the surviving badges, especially costly and difficult to produce, requiring three partners to invest heavily in a secretive and risky venture? Perhaps in this case it is permissible to speculate (like those biographers who were permitted to see printed books in Gutenberg's vague tinkerings of the 1430s) in a direction that likewise is not yet bound by evidence: is it possible that Gutenberg managed to invent 'magic' mirrors that did not utterly fail in their pious purpose? What if they actually succeeded in reflecting a stored image of the Aachen relics? As everyone knows, when a highly polished surface is directed towards sunlight, even accidentally, a corresponding pool of reflected light can be projected at an angle onto a darkened wall. Suppose, then, that an inventive artisan polished only certain areas of the metal to an even higher degree of reflectivity, creating a contrasting, even brighter pattern, say, in the shape of the Virgin Mary's gown; then, perhaps, back home again, on a sunny day, the pilgrim could select a well-shaded wall on which to project a glowing apparition of that holy relic, just as it had been 'captured' at Aachen, thereby fulfilling the mirror's devotional functions of retention and conveyance not merely in the pilgrim's pious imagination, but for all to see. If only such a thing had survived.

In the years 1444 to 1448, during which knowledge of Gutenberg's whereabouts and activities remains elusive, the city of Mainz underwent a radical change – if not for the better, then at least for the more peaceful. A resolution was ratified in December 1444 that granted eligibility for election to the city council only to members of the craft guilds. Patricians were not excluded outright, but in order to qualify for the council they simply would have to become guild members and then be elected from the guild ranks; as it happened, no patrician earned election. This reconfiguration of the council was engineered by Dr Conrad Humery, a canon lawyer who had served for several years as the old council's legal advisor; on the strength of his distinguished service and staunch anti-patrician views, he was appointed Chancellor of the new city council. Yet even the unanimous voice of the new council could not effect the desired reduction of the mounting municipal debt, or impose any taxation on the Church or its patrician appointees; moreover, all citizens still had to swear allegiance to the archbishop in the event that armed conflict came to the region.

Gutenberg was back in Mainz in October 1448, borrowing money, and something of a stranger in his own hometown. As if to provide clarification (or a reminder) of who he was, the 1448 loan document refers to him as *Henn Genssefleisch, den man nennet Gudenbergk* ('whom one calls Gutenberg'). Indeed, who was this middle-aged man who finally returned to Mainz? Although it is impossible to draw a true portrait of Gutenberg's character out of a handful or two of random legal documents, and perhaps too easy to conclude from them that he was a litigious boor, clearly he was *different*. He did not fit comfortably into the patrician norms in terms of career and behaviour; he moved along the periphery of various social and professional orbits without ever landing firmly within them; he left his home and returned again after a busy decade or so, never having remained with any partners or friends for long; he steered clear of a life in the Church and dodged the prospect of marriage for as long as he lived; and he achieved small feats of invention that dazzled prospective investors but left them wanting something more. Although the portrait of Gutenberg that emerges in these early stages may seem hopelessly indistinct, it appears to be consistent with what can be learned of the man from the vague but more pertinent documents of the following decade.

THREE

In Golden Mainz

At a forgotten moment that subsequent chroniclers recalled vaguely as '*anno* 1450', Gutenberg conceived of an exciting new project in Mainz. It was not simply another attempt at pilgrim mirrors or some other known pathway to profit, but something entirely new, based on a fresh invention, sufficiently important that later chroniclers would memorialize it with praise and gratitude. Gutenberg knew that if this new start-up was going to succeed, then he was going to need to have much more money at hand than the 150 florins that he recently had borrowed from Arnold Gelthus, or what his own annual annuities could provide. His supplies would be fearfully expensive, and he would need ample space, skilled workers and enforceable secrecy. To this end, he was already confiding in Johann Fust of Mainz, a man about whom history is even more secretive than it is about Gutenberg. Fust is often called a banker, without any evidence, or a goldsmith, which is simply incorrect (his brother Jakob Fust was the goldsmith). All we know about Johann Fust is that he lived in Mainz, he was not from a noble family, he nevertheless had access to large amounts of capital (presumably a lot more than the patrician Gelthus could offer), and after his dealings with Gutenberg came to an end in late 1455 he would continue to head a successful printing operation for about a decade; he died during a trip to Paris in 1466.

By mid-1450 Gutenberg had some promising results to demonstrate for Fust, who recognized enough potential in them to commit to parchment a legal agreement involving a substantial loan. But here the chickens must be separated from the eggs: had Gutenberg invented something ingenious in solitude, which he then pitched to local investors like Fust, hoping they might help him realize its potential? Or had Fust envisioned a new opportunity for profit in the abstract, and recognized in Gutenberg the one man who could give it physical form? Other undocumented scenarios are possible: Gutenberg or Fust may have rounded up other investors, such as acquaintances from Strasbourg or Eltville, each of whom may have brought workmen and supplies. In any case, the only one of Gutenberg's potential investors who happens to be documented is Johann Fust, and Fust's role in the partnership must be defined by what he could bring to the table. He was not an inventor but a capitalist, a money manager who would supply a major part of the funds that Gutenberg would use to develop the unnamed apparatus upon which the joint venture depended. The initial agreement between Gutenberg and Fust does not survive, but a court document drawn up five years later summarizes the essentials: during the summer of 1450, if not earlier, Fust had agreed to supply Gutenberg with the impressive sum of 800 florins – roughly the value of a hundred meaty oxen, or perhaps four sturdy working-class houses in Mainz – borrowed at 6 per cent annual interest (itself equal to two craftsmen's annual wages), with at least some portion of Gutenberg's equipment standing as collateral in the event of a default. Clearly, both men felt the undertaking was worth substantial risk.

The joint enterprise was the making of many books. The need for greater speed in the creation of books was a problem that every generation in every kingdom had faced. Whether it was Gutenberg, Fust or someone else who initiated the urgent push for its solution in Mainz around the year 1450 is a detail lost to history. Nevertheless, before long, Gutenberg had devised a method of arranging inky letters on a page, and an ambitious but secret programme for the multiplication of books was now the singular goal. By 1452 the results of his work must have been quite exciting, enough to overcome fears of rising expenses and risks. In a second agreement with Gutenberg, appended to the first, Fust personally invested another 800 florins, not as another loan, but in instalments that would begin at 300 florins annually, all at his own risk 'for their joint profit'. At this point the project had expanded beyond the development of Gutenberg's apparatus; it expressly involved ink, paper, vellum (parchment), workmen's wages and Gutenberg's supervision of the *werck der bücher* – the 'work of the books'.

From what we know of Gutenberg's prior experiences and historical reputation, the invention of the process, the building of the apparatus and the tasks related to running it fell within his domain. The special black ink may have been another of his inventions, but not the paper or the vellum. Those were costly commodities that anyone with sufficient funds could bring to the partnership. Instead of duplicating Gutenberg's skills, or those of a young calligrapher that Fust brought onto the team, Fust or some other unseen partner would have represented a particularly valuable asset if he knew how to import vast quantities of paper, had at his disposal several thousand head of cattle whose skins could be harvested for the vellum, and knew something about trade routes, transport and markets abroad.

The first fruits of Gutenberg's experiments with inked types and paper, no doubt faulty but encouraging, have not survived. Likewise, no original types, printing presses, typecasting tools or first-hand records concerning the 'invention' of printing in Mainz exist from the 1450s. However, several unique, mysterious and often fragmentary survivals of minor or ephemeral printed texts demonstrate that typographic printing in a developmental stage was circulating in and around Mainz during the early 1450s. A meagre fragment preserving roughly fourteen verses of an anonymous German poem known as the *Sibyllenbuch*, found in in Mainz in 1892 after serving for centuries as a scrap of recycled paper within an archival binding, appears to be the most primitive of all European typography (illus. 16). It is strictly undatable, but a very early stage of development is indicated by several typographic faults and experimental dead-ends that would disappear from the earliest securely datable European printing, produced with similar materials in 1454 and 1455. The poem in its longest form (as it is known from fourteenth-century manuscripts) could have extended to 1,040 rhyming verses, which, given the pace of 28 verses per page established by the extant fragment, would have required 37 or so printed pages: that is, both sides of nineteen or twenty leaves of a quarto booklet about the size of a modern theatre playbill. However, since all that survives of the Mainz *Sibyllenbuch* is the retelling of the Last Judgement, specifically verses 703–19 and 732–46,

16 *Sibyllenbuch* fragment (Mainz, c. 1452?).

the evidence therefore testifies only to the much shorter version of the text known to end at verse 748, which would make the Mainz fragment the final leaf of a fourteen-leaf pamphlet. This might seem a modest undertaking, but at the time it was ambitious, and a stack of these little books would have been impressive enough to convince investors like Fust that even greater things soon would come to fruition.

The text of the *Sibyllenbuch* was a tour-de-force of folklorish embroidery upon biblical themes, with two-thirds of the poem looking to the biblical past while the middle third wove a grand prophecy of how the end of time would unfold for the Holy Roman Empire. It begins with the history of the holy wood of Christ's True Cross, from the planting of a tree upon Adam's gravesite to its use as a wooden plank in King Solomon's bridge by the walls of Jerusalem, where the Queen of Sheba proves its miraculous properties. The second section recounts the sibylline prophecies in which Christ will be born of a virgin; how the German emperor Frederick Barbarossa, lifeless for centuries in the Kyffhäuser in the hills of Thuringia, will reawaken to recapture Jerusalem and convert all infidels to Christianity; how the Christian world empire will collapse at the hands of the Antichrist, whose evil deceit and oppression will finally be undone by the prophets Enoch and Elijah; and, as portended by 'fifteen signs', how Christ will return to conduct the Last Judgement. Another section, omitted from various manuscripts and probably not included in the Mainz pamphlet, added the further history of the Cross up to the time of Christ's crucifixion, concluding again with the Last Judgement.

Although the particular circumstances of the printing of the *Sibyllenbuch* are long forgotten, the rhyming couplets that Gutenberg set down in type were not intended to be read by someone sitting alone in silence at a desk. They are reflections of the oral culture of medieval Germany, meant to be read publicly, out loud, to listeners who were deeply concerned about what the heavenly plan might hold for true Christian believers under the new Holy Roman Emperor, Frederick III. Clearly, European printing had a connection to daily life from the very beginning. Interrupted by losses, the text of the *Sibyllenbuch* fragment reads:

leben Und mußen do hien do got urtel wil
geben Sie gene mit schrecken dohien Die
got nye erkanten noch forchten en Niemand
mag sich verbergen nicht Vor den gotlichen
angesiecht Cristus wil do urtel sprechen
Und wil alle boßheit rechen Die nie ge-
daden den willen sin Den wil er geben ewige
pin Und wil den guden geben By ym freude
und ewig leben Siit die werlt und alle ding
Die in der werlt geschaffen sint Czugene
und werden auch zu nicht Als man wol

[thirteen verses wanting]

er werden von pine erlost • wer in dem hymel-
rich ist Der hat freude mit ihesu crist Der
von dem hymel her nidder ist kommen Und
mentschlich natuer hat an sich genommen
Und an der mentscheit ist erstorben Und mit
dem dode hat erworben Daz wer do glauben
hat an en Mynne und zuversiecht der sal zu
ym • wir sollen gantzen glauben haben Daz
wir von ihesu crist horen sagen Und sollen
alle unser werck und syne Czu xpo keren yn
liebe und yn mynne Und zu ym haben zu ver-
[sicht]

[All] must go before God to be judged;
They shall pass before him in trembling,
Who never acknowledged nor feared him.
None may hide/ From the divine countenance. Christ
wishes to pronounce his judgement
And to avenge every evil./ Those who subverted his will
Shall be given eternal torment/ And to the good
He shall give joy and everlasting life by his side.
That are created in this world
Shall pass away and come to nothing/ As one well . . .

. . . he will be delivered from torment.
Whoever is in the kingdom of heaven
Is filled with joy beside Jesus Christ,
He who descended from heaven/ And took human form,
And on behalf of humanity met with death,
And with his death has earned That those who believe
will grant him/ The faith and love that is due to him.
We should have wholehearted belief In all we
hear told of Jesus Christ,
And devote all our work and thoughts
To Christ in love and devotion,
And have trust in Him.[1]

It is a clunky printing of poetry, with run-on lines, but it
works. The 26 capitalized words demarcate new verses – these
were helpfully highlighted in red ink soon after the printing,
proof that the pamphlet was used – and every word that precedes
a capitalized word creates a rhyming couplet with the final word
of the following verse (*leben/geben*, and so on). There is no punctuation except in the case of full stops terminating the two
verses that precede what should have been a capital W, which
was not available; similarly, there was no capital Z, so Cz was

used. These are clues that this early typeface was created for printing Latin texts (which lacks the letter w), not German. Nearly every word ending in -*en* or -*em* has been abbreviated, as have all but two of the occurrences of *und* as well as four instances of *der* and three of *ver*-, among others.

Gutenberg's typeface for the *Sibyllenbuch* closely imitated the bold Gothic script that contemporary scribes labelled as *textus quadratus* in the samples of scripts that they wrote out as advertisements of their skills. It is a highly formal script that long had been used by scribes for Bibles and liturgical books such as missals (for the Mass) and psalters (for reciting the psalms). The script's parallel vertical strokes, with sharp quadrangular serifs, were written at regularly spaced intervals, all contributing to a continuous rhythm and an overall 'woven' appearance. Numerous rules for combining letters (ligatures such as ß, æ and fi) and modifying abutting pairs of letters that 'face' each other (such as ra and ed) maintained a close-knit visual unity and made this a complex but extremely handsome script. Many of the minuscule letters of the *Sibyllenbuch* typeface have a secondary abutting form, in which the left side was flattened by removing any serifs or spurs, so that the letter could rest contiguously against the preceding letter. For example, in the combination 'eb', the projecting thorns on the back of the b were removed so as not to collide with the rightward extensions of the e (later Mainz printings would dispense with these thorns entirely). However, whereas a scribe would allow the extended parts of consecutive letters to overhang or to invade each other's unoccupied area, as in the combination ſz, the types of the *Sibyllenbuch* permitted no such kerning. Each letter occupies a horizontal range that is exclusive unto itself, so that the ſz in 'boſzheit' is rendered as two separate nonimpinging type sorts: 'boſ zheit' (recto, line 6). Subtle flaws such as this, which undermine the intended rhythm of the script, were corrected in slightly later printings. In time Gutenberg would provide a capital W sort and dispense with the awkward letter t with its overly long crossbar. Clearly, the creation of the first European typeface was not a single invention, but a process of development.

The metal letters Gutenberg invented have long been known as 'moveable types', and indeed they needed to be independently interchangeable. Unlike in blockbooks, nearly every letter of the printed *Sibyllenbuch* text is the ink impression of a single cast piece of type, each with its own particular height and width. The few exceptions are the fused types dê, do, ff and ft. But to print properly, moveable types have to remain immobile, locked in straight alignment. To accomplish this their printable surfaces could be of varying widths (compare the letters i and m), but their vertical measurement had to fall between the extremities defined by the roofline of the ascenders atop the letters b, d, f, h, k, l and t, and by the basement of the descenders below the letters g, j, p, q and y. Meanwhile, the capital letters could be very wide, but only as tall as the combined height of the ascenders and descenders. Finally, the metal shafts of type, just long enough to be grasped between agile fingers, needed to be cast to precisely the same standing height, so that the types presented a uniform surface upon which ink and paper engaged evenly. In the printing of the *Sibyllenbuch* this precision was not yet possible: the types do not march in lockstep, as they remained all too moveable – imperfect casting allowed the type heights to be uneven, causing poor inking, and their pronounced wobble suggests that their shafts were not cast to a perfectly straight rectangle. Moreover, the casting was rougher than would become the accepted norm, resulting in highly variable and imprecise letter forms. But the oil-based printing ink – another crucial invention – was uniformly black, homogenous in texture and quick-drying enough to be resistant to spreading or smearing.

This was the state of the art of Gutenberg's earliest known typographic invention, the first among several.

Physical remains or descriptions of Gutenberg's type manufacturing process do not survive. Later generations of European printers, beginning perhaps just after Gutenberg's death, were able to chisel a hard steel positive (protruding) punch for each letter, which then was driven into a softer metal to form a permanent negative (hollowed) matrix for the shape of the letter, into which a molten alloy could be poured by means of a casting mould, creating by repetition hundreds of identical types with the shape of the letter raised in relief. But closer examination of Gutenberg's types shows that they are *not* identical, and do not descend from a single matrix made from a single punch. The constituent elements of the same letters in his fonts were built up in inconsistent relationships to each other: their bows and crossbars swell and shift; the dots of the letter i wander in relation to their shafts. Each letter seems to have been shaped by means of the manual impression of individual tools for each shaft or serif or dot in a medium much softer than metal, much like a scribe writing cuneiform in clay, and each unique sort was then cast from its own temporary mould. This forgotten, perhaps counter-intuitive method of type production appears to have been an early experiment that succeeded well enough, but which took so much effort that later printers were eager to abandon it. Then again, it is a hallmark of the ingenious nature of Gutenberg's technical exploration that to this day nobody knows exactly how he did it.

Pictures of printing presses began to appear three decades after Gutenberg's death. The earliest that is known, printed in a *Danse macabre* that was illustrated with woodcuts at Lyon in 1499 (illus. 17), shows the very moment when Death, who eventually comes for all walks of life, visits the workplace of a trio of doomed printers. Unfortunately for curious onlookers, the work of the press is not proceeding as usual. The compositor sitting at the left, pulling types from the lower case, has been interrupted by a skeletal intruder. Normally, he would load his hand tray with one line of selected types and spacers and set it into the larger wooden forme that rests on the bench beside him, eventually composing whole pages of type. In the middle of the scene, another animated corpse harasses both the 'beater' who inks the type formes with stuffed leather pads and the suitably burly fellow who pulls the bar of the large wooden press. The latter victim is standing precisely where one would prefer to see the portion of the press that did the actual printing, where, presumably, the turning of the screw caused a flat metal platen to descend (somehow *without* turning) upon a single sheet of paper loaded into the folding box-shaped frame below. This downward force engaged the paper with the inked forme of

17 Death visits the printing shop, woodcut from *Danse macabre* (Lyon, 1499).

types, creating one impression of a single page at a time. At the right a bookseller, too, meets his untimely end with much too much inventory remaining unsold.

Perhaps the least noticed aspect of the 1499 Lyon woodcut is the single glazed window above the compositor's desk. Windows were essential in early printing shops, as daylight determined the working hours, and time equalled money. The shop also needed access to water, as the paper needed to be dampened before printing, and ample space was necessary to hang up the hundreds of identical printed sheets to dry overnight. Clear passage from the compositor's desk to the press was essential, as the composed metal type formes were very heavy, and the press required its own elbow room to allow the paper handler and the beater of the ink to stay out of each other's way. The puller of the bar likewise needed enough clearance to put his back into his sweaty, repetitive work – his was a beast of a job, not for someone's little brother to try. Mingling with the aroma of fresh paper were the odours of the oily inks, labouring men and, most pungent of all, the urine for cleansing the ink from the used types and ink pads. All day long, the rhythmic creaking of the press accompanied the pressmen's murmured chanting as they called out their readiness for the next step of their endlessly repetitive and difficult dance.

It is not known where Gutenberg's printing shop was located. His places of residence in Mainz are not documented, and even if they were, nothing requires that he would have set up printing presses in his home. Just as his choice to reside in the St Arbogast district outside of Strasbourg may have reflected a desire to work without municipal restrictions, strictures on labour practices within Mainz may have led him to select a workplace just beyond the walls of his home city. Indeed, when in 1471 the Sorbonne professor Guillaume Fichet penned his florid praise of Gutenberg's novel art, he located its birthplace as 'not far from the city of

Mainz'. In this regard it is noteworthy that in 1457 the *Liber fraternitatis* of the church of St Viktor recorded that Gutenberg was a benefactor and member of its lay confraternity. Situated near the Rhine about a mile southeast of the walls of Mainz, St Viktor was home to well-connected, influential canons who may well have recognized the international value of printed texts from the very beginning. The school of St Viktor, where Gutenberg's second cousin Jacob Gensfleisch served as master in 1439, had perennial need for lesson books, and at least one edition of indulgences was printed locally for the Dean of St Viktor in the 1460s. Moreover, the spacious church precinct could well have accommodated Gutenberg's first printing shop; a subsequent printer, Franz Behem, set up a press at St Viktor and in 1541 published the *Encomion chalcographiae* of Johannes Arnoldus Bergellanus, one of the most well-informed sixteenth-century accounts of Gutenberg's work.

Even before Gutenberg started the *Sibyllenbuch*, he probably had printed an edition or two of the *Ars minor*, excerpted from the teachings of Aelius Donatus, the fourth-century CE Roman grammarian and mentor of young St Jerome, which became the standard introductory Latin grammar used in northern European schools (such as that of St Viktor) during the later Middle Ages. Gutenberg was motivated to print the 'Donatus' at the outset of his work because the continuous demand for it in schools across the Holy Roman Empire ensured its commercial viability. Used by schoolboys year after year, these schoolbooks never lasted very long, and no one shelved them in libraries. When they survive at all it is as mere clippings of spare vellum that later fifteenth-century bookbinders recycled as liners or wrappers for more important books.

The earliest of all surviving Donatus editions appears to be the one preserved as two vellum binding fragments in the Universitätsbibliothek in Darmstadt (illus. 18). Its text originally

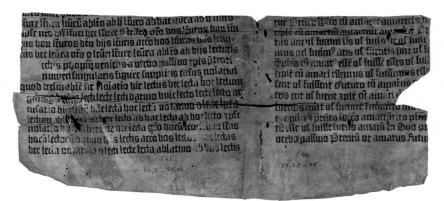

18 Donatus, *Ars minor* fragment (Mainz, *c.* 1453).

featured 27 lines of the *Sibyllenbuch* types per page, arrayed in
single wide columns across its fourteen leaves. Thus the printed
Donatus was not a small book, but rather a modest folio, six
lines taller per page and therefore substantially larger than the
Sibyllenbuch. Here the use of the tall Gothic types was intended
to familiarize the schoolboys with the *textus quadratus* that they
would encounter during a lifetime of reading from prayer man-
uals and liturgical books. As in the *Sibyllenbuch* fragment, the
type setting is uneven, dancing up and down when it should
march straight ahead, and the line endings are not yet well
justified, but the ink impression (that is, the evenness of the
height of each type) has improved markedly.

The Donatus text has eight parts and many subordinate
chapters. For the first time that we can actually see, the type
compositor demarcated the beginnings of sections by leaving
indented spaces for large initials to be coloured in later by
hand, and numerous two-line indentations for chapter initials
to be rubricated in red ink. It probably took only a few days to
print up several dozen of them. Once a few schoolmasters had
bought up the first editions, new editions could be set and
printed in short order, again and again, over the years. Scraps

from two dozen Donatus editions printed with these earliest
Mainz types and their gradually improved derivatives have survived, later discovered in early bookbindings from all over
Germany; many others must have disappeared entirely. They
represented a relatively easy way for Gutenberg to train novice
printers, to advertise the existence of his invention and to
maintain a steady influx of money.

Another printed Donatus fragment presents something of
a surprise and a puzzle. Discovered centuries later inside the
covers of a 1479 Basel edition of St Augustine's *De civitate dei*
that was bound at Seitenstetten in Austria (and now in the
Scheide Library at Princeton University), this Donatus was
printed not with the *Sibyllenbuch* types, but with a somewhat
smaller, narrower and much more elegant *textus quadratus* typeface composed in perfectly straight lines and with a notably even
ink impression (illus. 19). This brand new typeface, here in its
original and freshest state, would continue to be used in a subsequent, slightly altered state in directly datable works beginning
in 1454, a circumstance which suggests that this Donatus dates
from circa 1453, or perhaps 1454 at the latest. Here, for the first
time, we glimpse the admixture of Gutenberg's invention, Fust's
vision of success and the artistry of a new junior partner who
introduced fresh energy and indispensable talents: Peter Schoeffer
of Gernsheim.

19 Donatus, *Ars minor* fragment (Mainz, *c.* 1453).

Twenty or perhaps even thirty years younger than Gutenberg or Fust, Peter Schoeffer was still alive in December 1502 and still involved in a printing dynasty in Mainz that was continued by his sons and grandsons. He appears to have been educated at the University of Erfurt, where the enrolments record a 'Peter Ginsheym' in 1444 and a 'Petrus Opilionis' (Latin for shepherd, or Schäffer in German) in 1448. By 1449 the future printer was working as a calligrapher at the Sorbonne in Paris. There he proudly signed a manuscript of Aristotle's *Logica* in magnificent calligraphy: 'Petrus de Gernssheym alias Maguntina', thereby proclaiming his connection to Mainz (illus. 20). In November 1455 Schoeffer stood among Fust's closest associates in the legal documentation concerning the 'work of the books', and on 14 August 1457 he and Fust published their names as the printers of the Mainz *Psalter*, probably printed at the Hof zum Humbrecht, later known as the 'Druckhaus' (printing house). The *Psalter* introduced large ornamental red and blue printed initials and two extremely large and beautiful *textus quadratus* typefaces that much more closely resemble that of the 'Seitenstetten' Donatus than that of the *Sibyllenbuch*. Soon thereafter appeared a fancier-than-usual 35-line Donatus, printed with the same typeface as the 'Seitenstetten' Donatus. It featured large printed ornamental red and blue initials and a colophon stating that it had been produced by means of 'the new art of printing, that is, the making of characters, by Peter of Gernsheim in the city of Mainz, with his capitals, yet without the drawing of a pen'.[2]

What Schoeffer brought to Mainz, clearly, was genuine scribal artistry that neither Gutenberg nor Fust possessed. Therefore it is natural to see his return from Paris as a point of major transition in the development of typography in Mainz, wherein the broad, somewhat intransigent *Sibyllenbuch* types represented Gutenberg's first attempt at a *textus quadratus* typeface, while the more graceful and versatile types of the 'Seitenstetten' Donatus

20 Peter Schoeffer's
calligraphy, 1449 (now
lost), reproduced in
Johann Daniel Schöpflin,
Vindiciae typographicae
(1760).

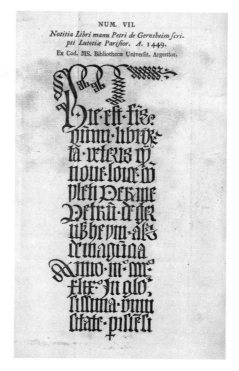

marked a conscious improvement made with the help of the new
man, Schoeffer. But a snappier-looking typeface was not the only
concern. Fust, the company bean counter, immediately appre-
ciated that whereas the *Sibyllenbuch* types could squeeze in only
27 lines per page of the Donatus, expending fourteen leaves of
vellum per copy, a Donatus printed with the svelte new typeface
comfortably accommodated up to 35 lines per page and required
as few as 10 leaves. Multiplied across entire editions, the significant savings in expensive raw materials, measured in many
hundreds of animal skins, could not be overlooked. Although it
meant creating a whole new typeface, such economizing would
pay dividends once the 'work of the books' escalated to the scale
that Gutenberg and Fust had envisioned when they first formed
their partnership.

One wonders how welcoming Gutenberg was to Schoeffer, a man half his age – clearly brilliant, and yet a mere copy-clerk – who offered bright new ideas for improvements upon his inventions. Fust, meanwhile, was delighted with the young man's contributions and treated him like part of the family. The older inventor eventually recognized that he had to adapt so that the work could move forward. With the benefit of Gutenberg's experience and Schoeffer's skill, the team made excellent progress on the new type design and soon great quantities of metal (some older types?) were melted down so that more and more of the newer typeface could be cast. Gutenberg could do as he wished with his old *Sibyllenbuch* types, but the all-important 'work of the books' was going to proceed with the next generation of types. Meanwhile, Fust and any other partners were busy negotiating the largest aggregate purchase of paper up to that point in European history, making the most of their business contacts abroad while notifying local parchmenters that calfskins prepared for the making of large folio books would be needed by the thousands. A great day for Christianity was aligning in the stars over Mainz.

Then, on Tuesday, 29 May 1453, following a 53-day siege that saw a portentous lunar eclipse in its final week, Constantinople – the capital of the Byzantine Empire, the seat of the patriarch of the Eastern Orthodox Church and the strategic gateway between East and West – fell before the cannons of Sultan Mehmed II. News of the death and decapitation of Emperor Constantine XI Palaeologos, widespread civilian slaughter and the collapse of Christendom in the East reached the Republic of Venice on 29 June; Pope Nicholas V in Rome was informed on 8 July and Emperor Frederick III heard the grave news in Graz on 12 July. Throughout Europe, shrill calls for a new crusade against the Turkish 'infidel' ensued, as did the casting of blame for allowing such a disaster to occur. In German towns such as Mainz, two

kinds of fear took hold of the Christian populace as it con-
templated what on Earth might happen next: fear that a mortal
and seemingly unstoppable enemy was marching towards their
borders, and fear that the Day of Judgement might be near. How
could one help prevent further catastrophes and make spiritual
amends in the eyes of a displeased Saviour?

The earliest date that is firmly associated with a specimen
of European printing, supplied by an unquestionable handwritten notarial entry, demonstrates that typographic printing
existed some time before Tuesday, 22 October 1454. On that day
in Erfurt, some 280 kilometres (175 mi.) northeast of Mainz, a
notary inscribed a small printed letter of indulgence for Margareta
Kremer and her son Johann, which survives today in fragmentary form at Princeton University's Scheide Library (illus. 21).
About a decade later, Hartung Kammermeister, the compiler
of the *Chronicle of Erfurt*, recorded the arrival of this indulgence
campaign as a local news item:

> In this same year [1454] a legate from Rome appeared
> in Erfurt, producing bulls from our Holy Father, Pope
> Nicholas v, which offered abundant grace; this same
> legate distributed letters to those who needed the
> indulgence, and he collected great amounts of money
> in the city and the countryside.[3]

The indulgences were produced for use in a Christian fund-
raising campaign that received the blessing of Pope Nicholas v
in Rome in 1452. It had been initiated on behalf of John iii de
Lusignan, King of Cyprus, at the request of Paulinus Chappe,
Cypriot ambassador, counsellor and administrator general. Also
known from twenty manuscript examples, the indulgence announced to all Christian believers that in an effort to defend
the island of Cyprus from Turkish incursion, all who made a

monetary contribution (according to their ability) would receive the pope's gracious permission to have local confessors grant them and their family members the fullest form of absolution and remission of sins throughout their lifetimes, and the plenary form of remission in their hour of death, provided that they genuinely repented and truly confessed their sins, and promised to fast on every Friday throughout one year.

The intention was that the indulgences would be available for three years beginning on 1 May 1452 and ending on 30 April 1455 – but there was a delay. Paulinus Chappe was not able to present his papal petition to Dietrich von Erbach, Archbishop of Mainz, until mid-1453, about the time that the disastrous news of Constantinople arrived, and then the archbishop took several months to confirm its authenticity with papal legates at the Diet of Regensburg. The first known manuscript copy of the indulgence was issued at Frankfurt am Main on 28 March 1454, but by then there were only thirteen months left in the window of validity, and even the hundreds of scribes within the archdiocese could not keep pace with the demand.

Purveyors of indulgences had always understood that their letter-writing campaigns would consume a lot of time, effort and money. Yet their indulgences succeeded, and public interest in them did not dissipate. One of these campaigns appears to have been staged in Mainz just prior to the instigation of the Cyprus campaign. On 2 May 1452 Cardinal Nicholas of Cusa wrote from Bruneck in the Tyrol to ask Heinrich Brack, prior of the Benedictines of St James in Mainz, for his assistance in the *expressio* of 2,000 copies of a new indulgence for Frankfurt am Main by the end of the month.[4] The need for so many indulgences within this daunting three-week deadline merely underlines the eternal problem faced by all such campaigns: in this case, could the monastery, or even the entire city, commit twenty competent scribes to the copying of indulgences for ten days, each at a pace of ten indulgences per day, to realize this demand? A lot of money (not to mention human salvation) was hanging in the balance, so one assumes that they tried their best. But there is no evidence that the Benedictines of St James felt it necessary to turn the task over to Gutenberg, or that he was quite ready to accept the work.

As for the Cyprus indulgences, a much bigger and broader campaign was envisioned. Beginning in the spring of 1454 and continuing through the summer, Gutenberg and young Schoeffer worked out the problem of rendering the indulgence text in very small types that could range with larger headings and even larger decorative initials. Once they had the text locked in place, proofed and approved, they could run thousands of small vellum sheets through the press; as the indulgences were compact and one-sided, the presswork was relatively easy. But here the typographer's involvement ended; once printed, the unfulfilled forms were retrieved by Church commissaries who attached Chappe's wax seal and distributed them by the wagonload to the priestly indulgence peddlers who did all of the travelling from town to town, preaching the spiritual benefits of penance and gathering money from people throughout the archdiocese. In addition to providing great spiritual comfort, if not true forgiveness of sins, the distribution of the indulgences resulted in the first widespread public exposure to the existence of typography. But what virtually no one perceived at the time was that the indulgences were the products of *two* printing operations, that is, two separate editions made with different materials.

Both editions of the printed Cyprus indulgences consisted of oblong vellum forms measuring roughly 20 by 28 centimetres (8 by 11 in.) each bearing headings in large *textus quadratus* types and the text of the indulgence in small rotunda types, with horizontal spaces left blank for the recipients' names, the place of issue, and the month and day to be written in by the priestly notary. In the first edition, consisting of 31 lines of text, the six headings were printed with Gutenberg's large *Sibyllenbuch* types, the ornamental initial for the first word (*Universis*) was V-shaped and the year was printed as 'Mcccliiii' (1454) early in the run, later updated to 'Mcccclv' (1455). Some 50 of these 31-line indulgences survive, mainly issued within the vast archdiocese of Mainz (illus. 22). In the second edition, however, a different small typeface was used to print the text in thirty lines. Here, the smaller *textus quadratus* typeface of the 'Seitenstetten' Donatus appeared in the six headings, the ornamental first initial was U-shaped and the year was printed as 'Mcccliiii' in one copy and as 'Mcccclquinto' (1455) in eight others that survive. These thirty-line forms were issued mainly within the archdiocese of Cologne and its surroundings, well north of Mainz.

This curious but mindful division of materials and labour clearly reflects two separate commissions from the Church. Although Gutenberg and Fust had pooled their resources for the ongoing 'work of the books', they appear to have worked independently on the indulgences, with one team led by Gutenberg using his own types to fulfil the immense commission of the Mainz campaign, while Fust, taking Peter Schoeffer to his side, accepted the slightly later and smaller commission from Dietrich II von Mörs, Archbishop of Cologne, using types developed after

21 Europe's earliest dated printing: 31-line Cyprus indulgence fragment (Mainz, 1454). Notarized 22 October 1454.

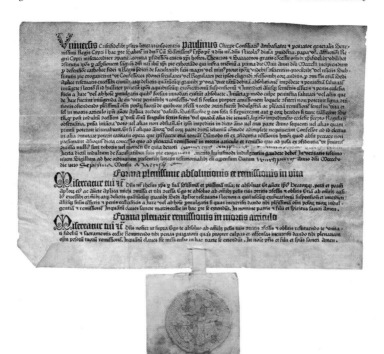

22 A 31-line Cyprus indulgence with seal (Mainz, 1454–5).

Schoeffer's arrival. Both parties would have been paid for the thousands of indulgences upon delivery, and both might have invested the money back into the joint 'work of the books'.

The Cyprus indulgences succeeded marvellously in demonstrating the commercial viability of a new technology, and yet on another level – through no fault of the printers – the campaigns would fail miserably: little or no military or monetary support actually reached King John III in Cyprus as various European authorities dipped into (or simply confiscated) the local indulgence proceeds; Paulinus Chappe himself was arrested in October 1455 on charges of embezzlement; and his head commissary in Erfurt, a Dominican friar named Johannes de Castro Coronato, who wrote out Margaretha Kremer's indulgence on 22 October 1454, soon fell victim to mental illness and was convicted of preaching heresy.

While the Cyprus indulgence campaign rolled along through the winter of 1454–5, Gutenberg's press continued to serve the causes of belligerence and fear in other ways. Certainly the most fanatical and downright peculiar printed survival from this period is *Eyn Manung der Cristenheit widder die Durken* (A Warning to Christendom against the Turks) (illus. 23). This slender nine-page pamphlet is, in one sense, a poetical calendar, arranged into twelve monthly sections that predict, in rhyming German, the time and date of each new moon during the year 1455. Given the medieval belief in the syzygy of the human body and the heavenly bodies, it provided a lunar calendar for medical treatments. But it also served as political propaganda, as each of the twelve months exhorted the temporal and ecclesiastical domains of Christendom to rise to Europe's defence against the Turkish threat during the imminent lunar cycle. This *'Türkenkalender'* was a useful almanac for self-care, particular to 1455, but with a jingoistic wartime tie-in. A familiar analogy might be a wall calendar from the Second World War that kept track of local rationing schedules, coupon values or necessary guidelines for civil defence, but which also featured monthly images that either energized the war effort or demonized the enemy.

In the pamphlet's rhyming couplets, January made its urgent appeal directly to Pope Nicholas v to make the Christian rulers set aside their internecine hostilities (a doomed hope) in order to unite against the Turks before the appearance of the new moon on the Saturday after St Anthony's Day, the nineteenth day of the month, at the tenth hour. February asked Emperor Frederick III to brandish his mighty sword by the morning of Ash Wednesday, 17 February. March implored David Megas Komnenos, the last Emperor of Trebizond on the Black Sea, and the princes in the Crimea, Albania, Bulgaria, Dalmatia,

Almechtig könig in hĩmels tron
Der uff ettrich ein dorne crone Vñ
sin streit baner uõ bludt roit Das heilge
crutze in sterbendõ not Selb hat getragẽ
zu d̄ mart' grois Vñ d̄ bitti dot nackt
vñ blois Dar an uumb mentschlich heil
gelittẽ Vñ uns do mit erloist uñ erstrickẽ
Vñ den bose fyant uõ wüdẽ hilff uns
vorbas in allẽ stüdẽ widd̄ unser fynde
durcken uñ heiden Mache en yren bosen
gewalt leidẽ Den sie zu cõstantinopel in
kriechẽ lant An manchẽ cristẽ mentschẽ
begangẽ hant Mit sahen martir uñ dot
slagẽ vñ ũsmehẽ Als den aposteln vor
zijtẽ ist gescheen Vmb die xij stucke des
heilgen glaubẽ gut Halt xij die gulden
zale in hut Auch werden dis iar xij nu-
wer schin Visiteren die xij zeichẽ des him
mels din Als mã zelet noch dñ geburt
offenbar M · cccc · lu · iar Siebẽ wochẽ

23 Eyn Manung der Cristenheit widder die Durken (Türkenkalender) (Mainz, 1454).

Croatia and Serbia to defend their contested fronts by noon on the eighteenth of the month. April turned to the kingdoms of France, England, Castille, Navarre, Bohemia, Hungary, Portugal, Aragon, Cyprus, Romania, Poland, Denmark, Sweden and Norway for help before midnight on 21 April. May preached the crusade to Europe's archbishops and bishops, setting a 16 May deadline. June called upon the Dauphin of France (later Louis xi) finally to make amends by 15 June for the violence that he and the Armagnac marauders had brought to Alsace in 1444. July reminded Philip the Good, Duke of Burgundy, that by the afternoon's third bell on 13 July, he should live up to the promise he made at the recent Diet to lead 60,000 troops eastward. August (with an unsightly misprint, repeating the last line of f. 3 recto at the top of the following verso) summoned the commitment of the Italian city states, especially the powerful fleets of Venice and Genoa, by early morning on 13 August. September petitioned Germany's seven great princes, electors of the Holy Roman Emperor, to defend the faith by the fourth hour after noon on 9 September. October invoked action by the eleventh day of the month from the dukes of Austria, Bavaria, Saxony, Braunschweig, Jülich, Guelders, Cleves and Silesia; from the margraves of Brandenburg, Baden and Meissen; and from the landgraves of Hesse and Thüringen. The following month charged the seven Free Imperial Cities (Mainz, Strasbourg, Basel, Speyer, Worms, Cologne and Regensburg) to join the fight by 9 November. Finally, December reported the 'glad tidings' of the recent conquest of three Ottoman strongholds in Asia Minor by İbrahim II Bey of Karaman, then called for a pan-Christian genocidal campaign, assisted from above by the Blessed Virgin Mary, to annihilate 'every last living Turk', whether in Turkey, Greece, Asia or Europe, by 9 December 1455 – all before wishing every Christian reader a Happy New Year.

Gutenberg did not write this inflammatory pamphlet, but he wasted little time agreeing to print it as soon as possible. Given that the text mentioned the Bey of Karaman's recent victories over the Ottomans, news of which reached the Diet of Frankfurt am Main on 6 December 1454, and that it concluded with cheerful wishes for the New Year, which fell on Christmas Day in Mainz, the writing and printing must have been done in mid-December 1454. As in several other contemporary lunation tracts, its 188 verses resonate with the Alsatian dialect, not that of Mainz, and the striking reference to the Armagnac incursions of 1444, which Gutenberg had experienced at first hand in Strasbourg, pinpoints the pamphlet's intended audience: Christians of Strasbourg and Alsace. Moreover, the anonymous author of the pamphlet was well informed about the recent news and specific talking points of the Diets of Regensburg and Frankfurt, such as the particular kingdoms and duchies involved and the details of Philip the Good's rash promise of troops. The confluence of evidence points to an Alsatian statesman and poet who had attended the Diet at Frankfurt in October 1454 as a member of the Strasbourg delegation, who, taking note there of the indulgences and Donatuses for sale, thought of another way to make use of Gutenberg's evident ability to multiply documents quickly.

In terms of typographic quality, the *Türkenkalender* of December 1454 reflects a significant improvement upon the *Sibyllenbuch* and the Darmstadt Donatus. Although its impression was still marred by uneven inking, especially (for unknown reasons) on the versos, the work featured sharper letter forms and straighter lines of text. Moreover, close analysis of the individual letter sorts in these works has revealed a gradual replacement of several of the odd forms found in the *Sibyllenbuch*, such as the b with the thorn on its back. Given these changes, the *Türkenkalender* has been defined as the first work in the 'second' state of Gutenberg's earliest types. The fact that this evolving typeface was used to print several editions of the Donatus, the *Türkenkalender* and two other ephemeral calendars, German bibliographers working in about 1900 designated what we have heretofore called the *Sibyllenbuch* types as the 'Donatus-und-Kalender' or 'DK' types (and so they will be referred to hereafter).

As the year 1454 came to an end, Gutenberg could look back upon remarkable and unprecedented accomplishments during the handful of years since his return to Mainz. He had conceived of a method of printing arrangeable metal letters and had demonstrated its practical applications with ever-improving results. He had convinced Johann Fust and others of the artistic quality and commercial viability of his invention, entering into a partnership that was deeply invested in an ongoing project of immense proportions. He had successfully published several texts for public consumption, showing the versatility and unbounded potential of his product, and had received an important commission for the printing of indulgences from the most powerful churchmen in the land. This final distinction not only brought him significant remuneration, but represented official validation of an essential premise of his work – that the rapid multiplication of desired texts offered great benefits to society. In the coming year, despite immense challenges and the most significant setback of his creative career, Gutenberg would achieve his greatest triumph by means of this new art, the one that would ensure his eternal fame.

FOUR

The Work of the Books

In October 1454, as the Cyprus indulgences began to flow forth from Mainz into the surrounding provinces, an Imperial Diet was held at Frankfurt, the next great city to the east of Mainz along the Main River. This was the second of three Diets that had been convened to rally commitments to an international 'crusade' to repel the forces of Mehmed II as they marched through the Balkans and along the Danube River towards Hungary and (it was now feared) the Imperial capital of Vienna. The keynote speaker at the Frankfurt Diet was Aeneas Sylvius Piccolomini, Bishop of Siena, Imperial Secretary and noted humanist writer, who in three and a half years' time would be elected pope under the name Pius II. At the first of the three Diets, held in Regensburg in May 1454, Piccolomini's stirring oration had called for 200,000 troops to recapture Constantinople within a three-year campaign. At the Frankfurt Diet in October 1454, Piccolomini confronted the German nobility's highly evident lack of commitment. Preaching the legitimacy, benefits and feasibility of the crusade, he assured the assembled diplomats that their princes had the means to defeat the Turks, and that victory therefore was only a matter of having sufficient will. Although Piccolomini had done his utmost, the main resolution of the second Diet was simply to reconvene for yet a third Diet, to be held in the presence of the heretofore absent Emperor Frederick III in Wiener Neustadt the following February. There, modest military aid was promised along the Hungarian front, but the news of Pope Nicholas v's death on 24 March 1455 put the international crusade – so urgently necessary the previous autumn – on indefinite hold.

While in Frankfurt, Piccolomini took note of something he had never seen before and wrote about it to his friend and colleague Juan de Carvajal, the Spanish cardinal of Sant'Angelo in Rome. Not quite five months later, having received an inquisitive reply to his first letter, he wrote again to Carvajal in Rome on 12 March 1455, this time from the Diet at Wiener Neustadt in Austria. Among other newsworthy topics, he mentioned again the spectacle that he had written about the previous October:

> Nothing false was written to me about that miraculous man seen in Frankfurt. I have not seen complete Bibles, but several quires belonging to different books, exceedingly clean and correct in their script, and without error, which Your Grace could read effortlessly, even without glasses. I learned from numerous witnesses that 158 copies have been completed, although some others say the number is 180. Of the quantity I am not entirely certain; of their completion (if one can have faith in informants) I have no doubt. If I had known of your wish, I should certainly have bought a copy. Several quires [of ten leaves] were sent to the Emperor here at Wiener Neustadt. I shall try, if possible, to buy a copy on your behalf and have it brought here. But I fear it will not be possible, both because of the distance and because they say that ready buyers had all been found even before the volumes had been finished.[1]

Overlooked by historians of typography until its rediscovery in 1982, Piccolomini's letter is the earliest European document that refers unmistakably to books being multiplied by means of typographic printing. It provides our only evidence of the original press run, and makes clear that the appearance of these new Bibles impressed discerning eyes for their precision and clarity, they were selling fast and excitement about them was already spreading across Europe. Yet the letter also leaves many questions unanswered. It fails to identify the 'miraculous man' who was selling so many Bibles at Frankfurt, and it sheds no light on the question of who had produced these Bibles or who had developed the new process of multiplying them.[2] Moreover, Piccolomini was unable to identify an individual or institutional sponsor of this miraculous project, such as the pope, the Archbishop of Mainz or the wealthy Benedictine Order. Instead, he had been left to believe that the source of all these handsome Bibles was a mystery man whose name he did not know. Thus, even from the very beginning, the reporting on these historic developments in Germany was fuzzy about the facts, and we are left to wonder whether there were indeed 158 Bibles, the lower but more specific figure cited by 'numerous witnesses', or more like 180, as 'others' claimed, a figure that seems suspiciously rounded off and possibly exaggerated. Either way, these were truly astonishing numbers, radically out of scale with Europe's available methods of manuscript production.

Clearly, the long-secret goal of the 'work of the books' undertaken by Gutenberg and Fust was the edition described by Piccolomini in 1455, known today as the 'Gutenberg Bible', which survives in some four dozen copies and various fragments (illus. 24). Its Latin text encompassed all of the accepted scriptures of the medieval Western Church, as translated from the original Hebrew and Greek by St Jerome from 382 to 405 CE, as well as an extensive set of individual book prologues that descended from Jerome and other sources. In addition to the canonical books of the Old and New Testaments, this 'Vulgate'

24 The Gutenberg Bible (Mainz, c. 1455), first leaf of Genesis.

version of the Bible included several apocryphal ('hidden') books that other traditions often chose to exclude: the third and fourth books of Ezra, Tobit, Judith, portions of Esther, the Wisdom of Solomon, Ecclesiasticus, Baruch, portions of Daniel, the Prayer of Manasseh and both books of Maccabees. Divisible into two volumes at the end of the Psalms, complete copies of this Bible consist of 643 leaves bearing 1,279 pages of text comprised of more than 3 million carefully ordered pieces of moveable type.

The first major book printed in Mainz is a large folio that was intended not for private study, but rather for reading at a lectern in a monastery refectory. It was printed on sheets of paper of a particular size called *Regal* (Royal), or on vellum (calfskin) sheets of the same size, providing leaves that measure about 41 × 30 cm. Royal was the second largest of the four traditional fifteenth-century paper sizes, among which only the Imperial size was larger; the two smaller paper sizes were Median (half the size of Imperial) and Chancery (half the size of Royal). 'Folio' format means that the book's sheets were folded once to create two attached leaves (bearing four pages); a book in quarto format used sheets that were folded again across the first fold to form a quire of four connected leaves, while in octavo format the sheets were folded a third time to form a quire of eight leaves. Generally, the Bible's printed sheets (bifolia) were gathered into quires of ten leaves.

Four major stocks of sturdy North Italian paper were used for the printing, each bearing the distinctive watermarks that served as the papermakers' trademarks: a main supply of bull's head paper (illus. 25), two varieties of clustered grapes and a running ox. Modern analysis demonstrates that the Bible's print-ers must have used up seven bales of paper with the bull's head watermarks, two bales containing an assortment of the two grape cluster papers and one bale of the running ox paper. These ten bales contained some one hundred reams (up to 50,000 folded sheets), enough to produce 130 or 140 paper copies of the 643-leaf Bible, allowing for mistakes and spoilage. At that rate, the printers would have expended some 6,000 calfskins to produce the three dozen or so vellum copies that completed the edition. The page layout of the first printed Bible is consistent with a layout that long had been familiar in the manuscript tradition. Nearly every page bears majestic twin towers of text, each one generally comprised of 42 lines of type. The printed area measures a little over 29 × 19 cm, which is very close to a sturdy 3:2 proportion. Moreover, to the naked eye, the columns are about as tall as the pages are wide, which creates a pleasingly balanced visual relationship. A hierarchy of variously sized indentations at the beginnings of the biblical books, prologues and chapters provided space for subsequent hand-illumination or decoration of the requisite initials; similarly, short spaces were left for the addition of chapter numerals by hand, while the empty upper margin was to be marked with the name of the particular book.

The men who had made 158 or even 180 of these Bibles must have seemed miraculous, indeed. Consider the prevailing economy of books, that is, the market for Bible manuscripts copied by hand: a precisely contemporary local example is provided by the 'Butzbach Bible', a 474-leaf folio Latin Bible copied out by the Brethren of the Common Life over the course of three years ending on 19 September 1454 for the Church of St Mark in Butzbach, 72 kilometres (45 mi.) northeast of Mainz (Giessen, University Library, Hs. 653). According to an inscription inside its back cover, the Butzbach Bible was completed at a cost of 21 florins and 2 shillings. This included 12 florins for the 'duplicating' of the scriptures by two scribes (one to write each volume), 6 florins for the illumination of the initials and borders, 2 florins for the paper and 1 florin for the two bindings. At a going rate of roughly 20 florins per unbound copy, Fust's

25 Bull's head watermark in the Gutenberg Bible (Mainz, *c.* 1454).

financial commitment of 1,600 florins to the 'work of the books' would have been equivalent to the cost of some eighty newly handwritten Bibles – and yet Gutenberg and his partners in Mainz had roughly double that quantity in mind. Moreover, they knew that if they succeeded in their work, which might well re-quire more than a year or two, it would not require that many months again just to create a second Bible, and a third one, and so on for many decades. They expected to emerge with 158 or more Bibles within the time it took to write only one. Significant profits loomed on the horizon.

Clearly the partners also had dared to dream that they might produce something much more beautiful than the somewhat cramped Butzbach Bible, which was the same overall size but was written hastily in a much smaller, informal, workaday cursive script. The upper limits of their artistic ambitions would have been defined by the splendiferous illuminated manuscript now

26 The Giant Bible of Mainz, illuminated manuscript, Mainz region, 1452–3.

known as the Giant Bible of Mainz, preserved in the Lessing J.
Rosenwald Collection at the Library of Congress in Washington,
DC (illus. 26). Comprised of 459 immense vellum leaves (57.6 ×
40.5 cm), this luxurious lectern Bible was made for the abbey of
Johannisberg, across the Rhine and just west of Mainz, at the
expense of Rudolf von Rüdesheim, dean of St Viktor near Mainz,
and Emmerich Nauta, abbot of the Johannisberg monastery.[3]
According to dated inscriptions, the anonymous scribe, who
called himself *Calamus fidelis* (faithful pen), wrote out the text
of the entire Latin Bible and its prologues and rubrics in two
carefully ruled columns of beautiful *textus quadratus* script during a fifteen-month campaign between 4 April 1452 and 9 July
1453. This magnificent work was the worthy textual ideal that
the printers hoped to approach, if not attain. Moreover, following long tradition, both the 'Giant Bible' and the new printed
Bible afforded ample opportunities for illumination, leaving
inset blank spaces for large historiated initials and a hierarchy
of smaller decorative initials, marginal extensions and lively
floral borders teeming with birds and animals. This is not to say
that Gutenberg sought to pass off his books as cheaper 'coun-
terfeits' of fine manuscripts. Even a quick glance at one of the
printed pages belies this silly (but indestructible) old notion.
As printed, still awaiting decoration to be arranged by the purchaser, Gutenberg's product could not have been mistaken for
a finished manuscript by that purchaser, and the text itself, lacking even the chapter initials, might have struck any attentive
contempary not only as unfinished, but as too impossibly tidy
and rigid to be mistaken for the work of a scribe, having somehow maintained the shapes, widths and heights of millions of
letters so that their differences are so minute as to be virtually
invisible to the naked eye – again, we can appreciate the 'miraculous' nature of that unnamed man in Frankfurt, whose Bibles
were so 'very clean and correct'.

The supply of metal type for the Bible project must have been immense, as well as appallingly expensive and laborious to produce. The printing of the Bible not only required more than 270 different varieties of type, encompassing upper- and lower-case letters, ligatures (fused letters), special abutting forms and punctuation, but each full page required about 2,600 letters. The work of the type compositors was unimaginably complex. Aside from the basic difficulty of rendering the sacred Latin text letter by letter (backwards, so that it would read left to right in print), the compositors had to observe innumerable special conventions for setting the abutting or overhanging letters and all kinds of abbreviations, taking pains never to conclude a column with a hyphenated word. The work inched along, line by line, column by column, page by page. Of course, the great difference between printed books and handwritten books was that whereas the scribe may have produced a single manuscript by the end of his many months of work, the miraculous men in Mainz could make an edition of scores or even hundreds of copies.

The distribution of four paper stocks within the Bible reveals a progression of use in which a large supply of bull's head paper was intermixed gradually with two grape cluster varieties, and, as supplies dwindled, was supplemented with the trotting ox paper in the final stages. Notably, this sequence of watermarks occurs not just once, but four times. These four parallel sequences reveal the working progress of four concurrent printing units as four teams of compositors sent formes of locked-up type to a small group of presses. The text was divided into four main parts representing roughly one half of each of the two volumes, ranging from Jerome's Prologue (f. 1r) through to the end of Ruth (128 leaves), and from 1 Samuel (f. 129r) through Psalms (196 leaves) in volume I; and from Proverbs (f. 1r) through Malachi (161 leaves), and from 1 Maccabees (f. 162r) through Apocalypse

(158 leaves) in volume II, respectively. One might elucidate the simultaneity of their work by means of a baseball analogy: after hitting the ball, the batter runs to first base while his teammate, already there, advances to second base; meanwhile, another man already on second runs to third, and the man who was there comes home to score. These four concurrent units completed most of the early quires, but as the work progressed, at least six different compositorial teams took on ever smaller sequences of text, substituting for each other and speeding progress as the final goal came into view.

The earliest of all quires to be printed, the first and fourteenth in volume I, both began with forty lines per column. The very first leaf commenced with the Prologue of St Jerome, which begins with a red-printed rubric, that is, a three-line title that explains that the introductory text is Jerome's letter to Paulinus of Nola (written in 394 CE) concerning all of the books of sacred history. This title is followed by a square indented blank space, six lines deep, that was left for the hand-decoration of a large capital F, the first letter of the Prologue, which begins with a mention of Jerome's friend St Ambrose, *Frater Ambrosius*. Towards the end of this prologue, the saintly translator invited Paulinus, and thus the reader of this Bible, 'to live among these books, to meditate upon them, to know nothing else, to seek nothing else'.

In the Bible workshop, the flow of corrected type formes to the presses was quite regular, probably adhering as much as possible to a pace of one page per day, that is, printing every copy of that page before sundown. An even number of presses must have been available: one or more presses were set up for the printing of the recto pages only, while their counterparts were for the perfecting of the versos. The printers did not necessarily keep four or six presses in action at all times, but that certainly would have provided for the smoothest possible workflow. One assumes

JOHANNES GUTENBERG   100

that the men were cross-trained in multiple tasks, so that the work was not halted when one of them took ill or needed time away. There are no reports of Death invading the first printing shop.

The first several pages of the Bible are as beautiful as printing would ever be. The contours of the types were sharp, their impressions were clear and the columns were spacious and even – the glorious first fruits from the happy innocence of Eden. Someone (Gutenberg himself?) even took pains to ensure that the first page of Genesis would end with the words *Viditque deus cuncta quæ fecerat, et erant valde bona* ('and God saw all that he had made, and behold, it was very good') – a celebration of work done well (illus. 27). The printers also provided the short but necessary rubrics at the beginnings of the Prologues, Genesis and 1 Samuel, each printed bright red by means of a separate inking and a second pull of the press. Some sheets no doubt were ruined when the registration of the second impression was imperfect, or the inking and masking went awry – but the risks were justified by the results. Or were they? Someone, more than likely Fust, pointed out that a few mistakes here and there, accumulated throughout the edition and across the dozens of book rubrics still to come, would add up to a major disaster in slow motion. Hundreds of sheets thus wasted could not be tolerated. A choice had to be made, and the decision doubtless caused a combination of distress and relief: the red rubrics would no longer be printed. Instead, spaces allotted for them would be left blank, for the eventual owners to fill in by hand as best they could. Therefore, the third composition team was told to commence Proverbs in volume II with a pair of entirely blank lines, sufficient either for the addition of the expected twelve-word titulus or for something shorter, as it happened to suit the rubricators who would be assigned to furnish them. Paradise no longer maintained its original perfection.

More adjustments followed. Whereas everything up through 'and behold, it was very good' and to the beginning of chapter 6 in 1 Samuel had been printed in spacious columns of forty lines, the lineation in Genesis was increased to 41 on f. 5 verso, with a new standard of 42 lines per column established on the following recto. Similarly, in the second composition unit, the 42-line norm was adopted on the eighth page of 1 Samuel. However, the columns did not get appreciably taller with the addition of two lines. Everyone in subsequent centuries who has pondered this silent adjustment has decided that it was done not for the sake of aesthetics, but for economy. Indeed, someone – one thinks first of Fust – had calculated that with some 1,250 pages yet to be composed, the introduction of a mere two additional lines per column would reap a savings of perhaps fifteen full sheets of paper or calfskin per Bible. Multiplied across the whole edition, this reduction was enough to provide surplus material for the printing of seven or eight additional Bibles, thereby offering significantly increased profit at no additional cost. Economy won the day, but page layout was not ignored. Limited by the platen, the columns with augmented lineation would have to fit within the same page proportions that previously had accommodated only forty lines. Gutenberg's workmen filed down (or by some other means lowered) the tallest of the Gothic pinnacles of the types so that lines of text would stack more compactly on top of each other. In their original state (represented by the 'Seitenstetten' Donatus fragment), the capitals and lower-case letters with ascenders or descenders had measured 7.3 mm in height. In this altered second state, the tallest letters were truncated to a maximum height of 6.9 mm so that columns of the same overall height as before could now hold two more lines. The difference between the first state of the types and the second is hardly noticeable, and so the hidden saving of reams of paper and vellum over the whole of the edition certainly could

libros diuisus ē. Monus ferex. Atqz
ita sūt pariter veteris legis libri viginti
duo: id ē moysi quinqz. et prophax octo:
agiographox nouē. Quamqz nōnulli
ruth et cinoch inter agiographa scri-
ptitent·et hos libros i suo putēt numero supputādos: ac p̄ hoc esse prisce legis
libros viginti quattuor: quos sub numero viginti quattuor seniox·apocalipsis
iohis inducit·adorantes agnū·et co-
ronas suas·p̄strates vultib; offerētes:
stantib; cora ꝗ̄uor aialib; oculatis
ante et retro id est in preterito ꝫ in futurū
respicientib;·et indefessa voce clamāti-
bus·sanctus·sc̄o·sc̄o·dn̄s deus omni-
potens·qui erat·ꝫ qui est·ꝫ qui vēturus
est. Hic plogus scripturax quasi ga-
leatū principiū·ōnibus libris quos de
hebreo vertim9 i latinū cōuenire potest:
ut scire valeam9 quidꝗ̄d extra hos est-
inter apocrapha ē ponendū. Igitur
sapia ꝗ̄ vulgo salomonis inscribitur·et
iħu filij syrach lib·ꝫ iudich·ꝫ thobias·
ꝫ pastor nō sūt i canone. Machabeox
pmū librū·hebraicū repi. Secūdus gꝛec9
ē:ꝗd ꝫ ipsa phrasi·pbari potest. Que
cū ita se habeāt: obsecro te lector·ne la-
borem meū rephensionē estimes auc-
quox. In reolo dn̄i·offert vnusquisqz·
ꝗd potest. Alij auꝫ et argentū et lapi-
des ꝓciosos:alij bissū et purpurā ꝫ
coccū offerūt ꝫ iacinctū. Nobiscū bene
agitur:si obtulerim9 pelles et capras
pilos. Et tamē apl̄s ꝫ contēptibiliora
nra magis necessaria iudicat. Vnde
et tota illa tabernaculi pulchritudo·ꝫ
p̄ singtas species ecclesie pūctis·futurox
distinctiō psalis regit ꝫ tilicijs: ardore
qz solis·et iniuria ymbriū·ea ꝗ̄ viliora
sūt phibet. Lege ergo p̄mū samuel.

et malachim meū. Meū inꝙ̄ meū.
Quicꝗd eni crebrius vertendo·ꝫ emen-
dando sollicitius·ꝫ didicim9 ꝫ tenem9:
nr̄m ē. Et cū intellegis ꝙd antea nescie-
bas·ut interpretē me estimato si grat9
es: ut paraphrasten si ingratus: quāꝗ
michi omnino ꜹscius nō sim·mutasse
me quippiā de hebraica veritate. Certe
si incredulus es·lege grecos codices et
latinos·ꝫ ꝯfer cū hijs opusculis ꝗ̄ nup
emēdauim9:ꝫ vbicūqz discrepare inter
se videris·interroga quelibet hebreox·
cui magis accōmodare debeas fidem:
et si nostra firmauerit·puto ꝙd ei nō
estimes ꝯiectorem:ut i eodē loco meū
sisuere diuinarit. Sed ꝫ vos famulas
xp̄i rogo ꝗ̄ dn̄i discūbentis p̄ciosissima
fidei mirra vngitis caput·ꝫ nequaꝗ
saluatorē queritis i sepulchro · quib;
iā ad p̄rem xp̄c ascēdit:ut orca lacran-
tes canes·qui aduersū me rabido ore
desceuiūt·et circueūt ciuitatē·atqz in eo
se doctos arbitrantur si alijs detrahāt:
orationum uestrax clippeos opponatis.
Ego sciens humilitate mea·illi9 semp
sententie recordabor. Dixi custodiam
vias meas:ut nō delinquā i lingua
mea. Posui ori meo custodiā:cū cō-
sisteret peccator aduersū me. Obmutui
et humiliat9 sū:ꝫ silui de bonis.

Incipit p̄m9 liber regū capitulū p̄mū

Vir vnus de ra-
machaim sophim
de mōte ephraim:
et nomē ei9 helcha-
na·filius ieroboā·
filij heliu·filij thau·
filij suph·ectaeus: ꝫ habuit duas vx-
ores:nomē vni anna:et nomen sc̄de
fenenna. Fueruntqz fenenne filij:anne

---

27 The Gutenberg Bible (Mainz, c. 1455), first leaf of 1 Samuel.

be considered well worth the effort. Yet in the eyes of Gutenberg and Schoeffer, who had worked so hard to give the types their original shapes, the call for increased lineation and the resulting alteration of the types may have been seen as a coldly calculated compromise of their artistic aspirations.

Several weeks (or about forty working days) into the work, all was going smoothly. The first composition team had proceeded through 32 leaves of St Jerome's prologues, Genesis and Exodus into chapter 8 (quires I:1 through 4). The second team had printed thirty leaves through 1 Samuel and into 2 Samuel, chapter 11 (quires I:15 and 16). Following the alteration of the types for 42-line columns, the third team had printed the second volume's first sixteen leaves, consisting of Proverbs, Ecclesiastes and Song of Songs into chapter 7 (quires II:1 and 2). By that time the fourth team had only recently started to print the opening page of 1 Maccabees, deep within the second volume (quire II:17). A total of 155 different pages had been printed, each more than a hundred times, not counting the inevitable wasted sheets. But by now the pressmen, or their employers, always mindful of maximizing returns, had noticed that more impressions of a single page could be made during a day's work than so far had been done; hours of useful daylight were going to waste.

Gutenberg and Fust began to entertain thoughts of expanding the edition size; even more Bibles would mean more buyers and more profits. Although significantly more paper and vellum would be expended as the work progressed, the extra cost would be offset by the possibility of selling more Bibles. It was decided to increase the number of copies to be printed by about a third, well beyond the original goal of perhaps 120 copies, so that from this point forward, for each sheet, roughly 30 or so additional paper copies and roughly another 10 or so on vellum would be produced, with a new goal of perhaps 160 or more copies. But what about the shortfall of all the early quires that all of the envisioned additional copies would require? The type-pages of Genesis, 1 Samuel, Proverbs and 1 Maccabees already had been sorted back into their type cases during the daily recycling that made new composition possible. Those pages would have to be reset and reprinted from the beginning once everything else had been completed (illus. 28). By that time the printers would have a much clearer view of what the successful press run was going to be. The course for the next two years of work was set.

Unbeknownst to Gutenberg, a few months after the decision to expand the edition size, a truly harmless little accident had occurred: a batch of black printing ink had been prepared that contained an unusually high ratio of copper to lead. The anomalous ink, used to print all of the copies of ff. 74 verso (Numbers 19), 114 verso (Judges 1), 201 verso (1 Chronicles 16), and 273 verso (Esther 2) in volume I, and f. 202 verso (Matthew 23) in volume II, looks entirely normal to the naked eye. But 530 years later the spike in the traces of copper on these pages (and no others) allowed nuclear physicists on the far side of an unimagined continent to determine that all six of these pages, from different parts of the Bible, had been printed with the same batch of ink on the same day.[4] This confirmed what previous modern bibliographical analyses of the watermarked papers had already suggested: at this point in the Bible, six composition units had worked concurrently on six different sequences of quires. Given the simultaneous printing of formes provided by multiple compositors, Gutenberg's workmen had expended nowhere near 1,279 days to print 1,279 pages, as one might expect, but more like 300 days of concurrent printing to complete the original setting, to be followed by an unknown number of days for printing smaller quantities of the 155 pages that still needed to be reset to fill out the increased edition size. With breaks on every Sunday and all major feasts, the otherwise constant creaking of screw presses and backbones may have consumed parts of only three years, stretching from 1453 into 1455.

The first composition team marched onwards through the rest of the Pentateuch, ending with the tenth quire, but they also printed the last two quires of Psalms to help finish off the first volume of the Bible, and took on responsibility for the Acts of the Apostles and the Epistles of James, Peter, John and Jude in volume II (quires II:29–31). After the second composition team proceeded through 2 Samuel, both books of Chronicles and the first two books of Ezra (quires I:17–24), they received help from other teams to finish off books 3 and 4 Ezra. Meanwhile, the third team laboured on the second volume, progressing through Ecclesiasticus and the major prophets Isaiah, Jeremiah, Baruch and Ezekiel (quires II:3–13). Concurrently, the fourth team continued with the latter portion of the second volume, printing 1–2 Maccabees, the Gospels and the Pauline Epistles through 1 Corinthians (quires II:17–26). At least two additional teams joined in to help complete what the other teams could not. When the third team commenced the New Testament (f. II:190r), a fifth team took over the printing of Joshua, Judges and Ruth (quires I:11–13) for team one, Daniel and the twelve Minor Prophets (quires II:14–16) for team three, and seven brief Pauline Epistles, ending with Hebrews (quire II:28), for team four. At that same time a sixth team took up the printing of Tobit, Judith, Esther, Job and the first 129 Psalms (quires I:27–31) for team two, as well as five of the Pauline Epistles (quire II:27) and finally the Apocalypse (quire II:32) for team four, all of which came to a perfect ending in the 42nd and final line of the final column on the final leaf.

However, everyone knew there was more work to do. After the teams finished their appointed tasks, they started all over again, resetting and reprinting the requisite number of impressions of Genesis 1 and the 154 other pages that had preceded

Jnapit liber bresith que nos genesim
dicim⁹ | Jn principio creauit deus celu
et terram. Terra autem erat inanis et
vacua: z tenebre erant sup facie abissi:
et spiritus dni ferebatur super aquas.
Dixitq; deus. Fiat lux. Et facta e lux.
Et vidit deus lucem cp esset bona : et
diuisit lucem a tenebris·appellauitq;
lucem diem et tenebras noctem. Factu
q; est uespere z mane dies unius.Dixit
quoq; deus. Fiat firmamentu in medio aquaru: et diuidat aquas ab a-
quis. Et fecit deus firmamentu : diui-
sitq; aquas que erant sub firmamento ab hijs que erant super firmamen-
tum: z factum est ita. Uocauitq; deus
firmamentu celi: z factum est uespere
et mane dies secundus. Dixit uero deus. Congregentur aque que sub celo
sunt in locum unu et appareat arida.
Et factum est ita. Et uocauit deus ari-
dam terram: cogregationesq; aquau
appellauit maria. Et uidit deus cp esset bonu· et ait. Germinet terra herba
uirentem et facientem semen : et lignu
pomiferu faciens fructum iuxta genus
sui : cuius semen in semetipso sit super
terram. Et factum est ita . Et protulit
terra herbam uirentem et facientem semen iuxta genus sui:lignuq; faciens
fructu et habes unuquodq; sementem secundum
specie sua. Et uidit deus cp esset bonu:
et factu e uespere et mane dies tercius.
Dixitq; aut deus. Fiant luminaria
in firmamento celi · z diuidat diem ac
nocte: z sint in signa z tepora· z dies z
annos: ut luceat in firmameto celi et
illuminet terra. Et factu est ita. Fecitq;
deus duo luminaria magna:luminare
maius ut preesset diei et luminare min⁹
ut preesset nocti· z stellas· z posuit eas in
firmameto celi ut lucerent sup terra: et

preessent diei ac nocti: z diuiderent lucem
ac tenebras. Et uidit de⁹ cp esset bonu:
et factu e uespere et mane dies quart⁹.
Dixit etiam deus . Producant aque
reptile anime uiuentis et uolatile sup
terram : sub firmameto celi. Creauitq;
deus cete grandia·et omne anima uiuentem atq; motabilem qua produxe-
rant aque in species suas: z omne uolatile secundu genus sui. Et uidit deus cp esset bonu: benedixitq; ei dicens.
Crescite et multiplicamini·et replete a-
quas maris : auesq; multiplicentur
super terram. Et factu e uespere z mane
dies quintus. Dixit quoq; deus. Pro-
ducat terra anima uiuentem in genere suo:iumenta z reptilia·z bestias terre secundu species suas. Factu e ita. Et
fecit deus bestias terre iuxta species suas: iumenta z omne reptile terre in genere suo. Et uidit deus cp esset bonu:
et ait. Faciam⁹ homine ad ymagine z
similitudine nostra·z psit piscibus maris·
z uolatilibs celi·z bestijs uniuersq; terre·
omniq; reptili qd mouet i terra. Et creauit deus homine ad ymagine et similitudine sua: ad ymaginem dei creauit illu:masculu et femina creauit eos.
Benedixitq; illis deus · et ait Crescite
et multiplicamini z replete terram · et
subicite eam: z dominamini piscibus
maris· z uolatilibus celi: z uniuersis
animatibus que mouentur sup terra.
Dixitq; deus. Ecce dedi uobis omne
herbam afferentem semen sup terram·
et uniuersa ligna que habet i semetipsis
semete generis sui: ut sint uobis i esca·
z cuctis aiantibus terre·omniq; uolucri
celi z uniuersis q mouetur in terra·et i
quibus e anima uiuens: ut habeat ad
uescendu.Et factu est ita. Viditq; deus
cuncta que fecerat : et erat ualde bona.

28 The Gutenberg Bible (Mainz, c. 1455), first leaf of Genesis,
2nd setting.

In principio creauit deus celu[m]
et terram. Terra autem erat inanis et
uacua: z tenebre erat super faciem abissi:
et spiritus d[omi]ni ferebatur super aquas.
Dixitq[ue] deus. Fiat lux. Et facta e[st] lux.
Et uidit deus lucem q[uod] esset bona: et
diuisit lucem a tenebris · appellauitq[ue]
lucem diem z tenebras noctem. Factu[m]
[que] e[st] vespere z mane dies unus. Dixit
quoq[ue] deus. Fiat firmamentu[m] in medio aquaru[m]: et diuidat aquas ab a-
quis. Et fecit deus firmamentu[m]: diui-
sitq[ue] aquas que erant sub firmamento ab hijs que erant super firmamen-
tum: z factum e[st] ita. Uocauitq[ue] deus
firmamentu[m] celu[m]: z factum e[st] vespere
et mane dies secundus. Dixit vero deus. Congregentur aque que sub celo
sunt in locum unu[m] et appareat arida.
Et factum e[st] ita. Et vocauit deus ari-
dam terram: co[n]gregationesq[ue] aqua[rum]
appellauit maria. Et uidit deus q[uod] esset bonu[m] · et ait. Germinet terra herba[m]
uirentem et facientem semen: et lignu[m]
pomiferu[m] faciens fructu[m] iuxta genus
suu[m]: cuius semen in semetipso sit super
terram. Et factum e[st] ita. Et protulit
terra herbam uirentem et facientem semen iuxta genus suu[m]: lignu[m]q[ue] faciens
fructu[m] z habe[n]s unu[m]q[uod]q[ue] sementem secu[n]dum
speciem suam. Et uidit deus q[uod] esset bonu[m]:
et factu[m] e[st] vespere z mane dies tercius.
Dixitq[ue] aut[em] deus. Fiant luminaria
in firmame[n]to celi-z diuidant diem ac
nocte[m]: z sint i[n] signa z tempora · z dies z
annos: ut luceat in firmame[n]to celi et
illumine[n]t terram. Et factu[m] e[st] ita. Fecitq[ue]
deus duo luminaria magna: lumiare
maius ut p[re]esset diei et lumiare min[us]
ut p[re]esset nocti: z stellas-z posuit eas i[n]
firmame[n]to celi ut luce[re]nt sup[er] terram: z

p[re]essent diei ac nocti: z diuideret[n]t lucem
ac tenebras. Et uidit de[us] q[uod] esset bonu[m]:
et factu[m] e[st] vespere et mane dies quart[us].
Dixit etiam deus. Producant aque
reptile anime uiuentis et uolatile sup[er]
terram: sub firmame[n]to celi. Creauitq[ue]
deus cete grandia-et omne anima[m] uiuentem atq[ue] motabilem qua[m] produxe-
rant aque in species suas: z omne uolatile secundu[m] genus suu[m]. Et uidit deus q[uod] esset bonu[m]: benedixitq[ue] ei dicens.
Crescite et multiplicamini-et replete a-
quas maris : auesq[ue] multiplicentur
super terram. Et factu[m] e[st] vespere z mane
dies quitus. Dixit quoq[ue] deus. Pro-
ducat terra anima[m] uiuentem in genere suo: iumenta z reptilia-z bestias terre secundu[m] species suas. Factu[m] e[st] ita. Et
fecit deus bestias terre iuxta species suas: iumenta z omne reptile terre in genere suo. Et uidit deus q[uod] esset bonu[m]:
et ait. Faciam[us] homine[m] ad ymagine[m] z
similitudine[m] nostra[m]-z p[re]sit piscib[us] maris-
z uolatilib[us] celi-z bestijs uniuerseq[ue] terre:
omniq[ue] reptili q[uo]d mouet[ur] i[n] terra. Et creauit deus homine[m] ad ymagine[m] et similitudine[m] suam: ad ymaginem d[e]i creauit illu[m]: masculu[m] et femina[m] creauit eos.
Benedixitq[ue] illi deus · et ait. Crescite
et multiplicamini et replete terram-et
subiicite eam: z dominamini piscib[us]
maris-z uolatilibus celi : z uniuersis
anima[n]tib[us] que mouent[ur] sup[er] terra[m].
Dixitq[ue] deus. Ecce dedi uobis omne[m]
herbam afferentem semen sup[er] terram-
et uniuersa ligna que habe[n]t i[n] semetipsis
semete[m] generis sui: ut sint uobis i[n] esca-
z cuctis a[n]imanbus terre · omniq[ue] uolucri
celi z uniuersis q[ue] mouentur in terra-et i[n]
quibus e[st] anima uiue[n]s: ut habeant ad
vescendu[m]. Et factu[m] e[st] ita. Viditq[ue] de[us]
cuncta que fecerat: et erat valde bona.

A 5.

29 The Gutenberg Bible (Mainz, c. 1455), first leaf of Genesis, a
replacement setting (similar to the second setting, with different
spacing around the punctuation), illuminated by the 'Fust Master'.

the expansion of the edition (that is, I:1–32r; I:129–58; II:1–16r; and II:162r) in order to make up the shortfall of total copies. Moreover, due to various accidents and oversights, a few of the copies, particularly the Morgan Library's Old Testament, turned out to be short one or two odd leaves. These were quickly perfected with newly composed replacement leaves, after which a two-leaf table of rubrics to serve as a guide for rubricators was printed up as a supplement. Finally, the sorted stacks of sheets were collated into the 33 distinct quires for volume I and 32 quires for volume II, and these quires were distributed into 158 or so stacks to make up complete Bibles. These were not sold as finished books bound in covers, but as complete sets of unsewn quires of folded sheets. Binding had to be arranged by the buyer.

At the time of its creation the Gutenberg Bible was the most common book in the Western world. Whereas every other European book before the mid-fifteenth century was a unique manuscript, or possibly from a small run of blockbooks, some 158 or more printed copies of this Bible were made available all at once for distribution to an equal number of churches, monasteries, universities, princes and prelates. Some copies stayed in Mainz: the Benedictines of St James and the Carthusians of St Michael each had copies. But most were destined for distant purchasers. Wrapped in rough paper and packed into barrels, many were rolled onto barges destined for riverfront landings up and down the Rhine or eastwards along the Main. Other copies were loaded into wagons for overland journeys that sometimes joined up with more distant riverways. While many of the Bibles were distributed to monasteries and churches throughout Germany, others found their way to Austria, Switzerland, France, the Netherlands and as far away as England, Spain, Denmark, Sweden, Bohemia, Hungary and Poland (there is no direct evidence of copies in Italy). Once the essentially identical copies reached their particular destinations and were illuminated, rubricated and bound, they became truly unique objects, full of evidence of their intended use and splashes of local colour. Whereas some of the Bibles, such as the copy now at the Biblioteca Nacional in Madrid and the very similar-looking Old Testament now at the Morgan Library (illus. 29), had been enhanced with hand-decoration in Mainz before export, others were dispatched to agents in Erfurt, Leipzig, Lübeck and Bruges, where they were decorated and bound in local styles, sometimes for export to clients still further afield. The fine vellum copy now in the State Library in Berlin was illuminated in Leipzig with more than four dozen historiated initials, that is, with pictures of St Jerome, the Creation, Moses, Joshua, Judith, Job, King David, King Solomon, Isaiah, Jeremiah, Daniel in the lion's den, Jonah emerging from the whale, the winged symbols of the four evangelists, St Peter and St John on Patmos, among others – much more pictorial content than the otherwise top-of-the-line 'Giant Bible' written and illuminated in Mainz in 1452–3 ended up getting. Then again, other printed copies had to settle for plain red and blue initials, given the limitations of the buyer's purse. Fust and experienced merchants of books and other wares probably took the leading roles in the long-distance sales and distribution, which doubtless exceeded the scope of Gutenberg's experiences and interests.

The Gutenberg Bibles would not have struck their fifteenth-century readers as something entirely novel or unfamiliar. They consisted of large, sturdy pages bearing in two columns the traditional collection of biblical texts transcribed in a familiar letterform. Moreover, once the text had been rubricated and bound into codex format between heavy wooden boards covered with tooled leather, the printed Bible was a passable substitute for a high-end manuscript Bible, only more affordable. Most of the new owners would have been less concerned with the Bible's outward appearances, or cost, than with the quality of its text. Signs of serious and extended use, such as lection markings or textual emendations and annotations, suggest that the Bibles fulfilled their functional expectations. Indeed, the first printed edition of the Bible succeeded in correcting one of the central deficiencies of the manuscript tradition: the textual variations, interpolations, omissions and errors that were the inevitable by-products of an imperfect process of handwritten transmission. The impossibility of copying truly identical texts had led St Jerome to complain in his prologue to Joshua that there were as many biblical texts as there were manuscripts (*tot sunt exemplaria pæne quot codices*); and so, with these words Gutenberg published the *raison d'être* of his Bible. Gutenberg and his colleagues did not seek to refine or purify the ancient texts – they were by no means biblical scholars – and therefore this first printed edition happened to contain some readings that were peculiar to manuscripts from the Mainz region, as well as some outright inaccuracies. However, for the first time readers in monasteries and universities across Europe could work with virtually identical Bibles and agree upon a uniform set of readings while knowing that their theological work and liturgical practices did not depend upon the accidents of local scribal work. The unprecedented textual uniformity provided by the first printed Bibles gave birth to the previously unheard-of concept of what is considered an 'edition' today: whereas two manuscripts might or might not convey identical or even similar information on any given page, it is the essence of the printed edition that it allows readers in many distant places to know and to agree that a certain passage on a certain page in a certain book reads, for better or for worse, the same way for everyone.

On 15 August 1456 a scribe in Mainz put the finishing touches to the rubrics, red and blue initials, chapter numerals, headings and captial strokes that he was entrusted to add to the finished sheets of the second volume of the newly printed

42-line Bible, which he then bound up and inscribed on the final leaf, just below the final printed words of the Apocalypse: 'This book was illuminated, bound and brought to completion by Heinrich Cremer, vicar of the Collegiate Church of St Stephen in Mainz in the year 1456, on the Feast of the Assumption of the glorious Virgin Mary, thanks be to God. Alleluia.'[5] Nine days later, on 24 August, the same rubricator completed the more difficult task presented by volume 1, which included the Psalms and their numerous headings and countless versal initials. He inscribed the final page of this volume beneath the 150th Psalm: 'And here ends the first part of the Bible, that is, consisting of the Old Testament, illuminated, rubricated and bound by Heinrich Albch, alias Cremer, in the year of our Lord 1456, on the feast of St Bartholomew the Apostle, thanks be to God. Alleluia.'[6]

Heinrich Cremer's work of rubrication at St Stephen's in Mainz, encompassing hundreds of rubrics and thousands of initials, must have taken several weeks to execute. Therefore, the printing of the 42-line Bible within the same city must have been completed before midsummer of 1456. The previous witness to the Bible's existence, Aeneas Sylvius Piccolomini, had written in March 1455 about the quires shown by the 'miraculous man' at Frankfurt am Main during the previous October, but he had been forced to rely on reports that the Bibles had indeed been finished in the meantime. A third document of relevance here – the sole source of information regarding the Gutenberg's 'work of the books' – was the so-called Helmasperger Instrument.[7]

This document was written and notarized by Ulrich Helmasperger following a session of the secular court of Mainz, which was convened at midday on 6 November 1455 in the refectory of the Barefooted Franciscans. The 'instrument' summarized a legal hearing in which Gutenberg and Fust had agreed to settle accounts and end their joint project. Fust, supported by his brother Jakob Fust, Peter Schoeffer and five other witnesses, sought repayment from Gutenberg of an immense sum of money: Fust's initial loan of 800 florins at 6 per cent annual interest over a period of more than five years (amounting to an additional 250 florins), and his infusion of a second 800 florins at the same interest rate over a period of nearly three years (amounting to another 140 florins), as well as 36 florins of compound interest that he owed his own creditors – a total of 2,026 florins. For some reason Gutenberg not only was late to the hearing, he was not coming at all. However, Heinrich Gunther, parish priest of St Christopher, Heinrich Keffer and Bechtolff (Ruppel) von Hanau had come to present a statement prepared by Gutenberg: essentially, 'Not so fast!'

Gutenberg's testimony stated, first, that Fust's loan was an advance on the cost of manufacturing a certain apparatus (*geczuge*) that would be Gutenberg's pledge as collateral on the loan. Second, the principal of the loan was not 800 florins, as Fust had provided only 750 florins, and Fust had given him a verbal waiver of the interest. Third, Fust had agreed to furnish additional sums of 300 florins annually to cover wages, domestic costs, vellum, paper and ink, and so on. This amounted to another 800 florins, for not quite three years of work, but this was not a loan at interest. Rather, it was Fust's capital investment as a partner in the joint venture, for his own profit and subject to his own risk. Gutenberg reasoned that he did not owe back money that Fust had used as his own investment, nor did he owe any compound interest. Finally, although Gutenberg had taken on other projects in the meantime, he had kept a close accounting of the money dedicated to the work of the books; in fact, he believed that he may have spent more than his share on it. He was prepared to show all of his accounting in order to prove his claims.

Still under oath, Fust realized that he had to backtrack, and so he revised his claim to only 1,550 florins, plus interest. At this

point, the court's judgement was that Fust would have to produce the written agreement concerning Gutenberg's responsibility for interest, and he would need sworn witnesses to
establish that his money in the venture was indeed borrowed
at interest. Meanwhile, Gutenberg would have to show the
accounting in support of his claims; if any more or less than 800
florins had been expended on their common venture, then the
proper amount would be added to or subtracted from the amount
he owed. Here Ulrich Helmasperger ended and notarized his
summary of the court hearing. It is one of the most telling documents in the history of early European printing, but also one of
the most confounding, as it stops short of revealing the final
settlement of the partnership.

For centuries, subsequent historians would spin romantic
tales of Fust's sinister betrayal of his partner Gutenberg – a devi-
ously timed scheme that the secular court blithely approved
– after which the bankrupted inventor had to stand by helplessly
as the parasitic Fust and Schoeffer called in more money than
he yet had to his name, and thereby took possession of the precious collateral on the defaulted loans: his printing press. Indeed,
Gutenberg seems always to have been short of ready cash. He
had borrowed 150 florins from Arnold Gelthus in Mainz in 1448,
perhaps because he was still in debt to his creditors in Strasbourg,
and in 1458 he began to default on his Strasbourg payments. But
if anyone had 'won' the court hearing of 6 November 1455, it
was Gutenberg. His testimony had cut down Fust's initial claim
by at least 50 florins and probably succeeded in reducing or elim-
inating the interest he owed. More important, Gutenberg had
exposed Fust's 'heads I win, tails you lose' misrepresentation of
his capital investment as a repayable loan, so that he had to repay not the whole amount, but only as much as he had *not* spent
on the work of the books. Thus Gutenberg probably owed Fust
no more than 750 florins and at worst five years' interest, perhaps

a total of 950 or so florins. Did this ruin him? He had expressed no concerns about his *ability* to repay what he acknowledged was Fust's due. He was still collecting various annuities, including payments of 26 florins from the city of Strasbourg during the Lenten fairs of 1453, 1454 and 1455. Even if he had not managed to establish a financial stake in the huge stock of Bibles that by 1455 were selling so quickly, he recently had delivered thousands of printed Cyprus indulgences to the Church – presumably a trustworthy paymaster. If his remuneration for that work did not suffice, he could always take out another loan (as penniless rich men well know). Then there was the matter of the collateral for the loan, an asset that Fust himself had tried to value at 800 florins. Fust was owed either the loan or the apparatus, not both. If Gutenberg repaid the loan and interest, the apparatus would be his; if he came up short of cash, he could cede the apparatus to Fust and owe nothing but interest.

After 1455 nothing more is heard of Gutenberg's partnership with Fust, and so his debts may have been settled then and there. As it happened, the types of the 42-line Bible remained with Fust and Schoeffer. Were the Bible types the major part of Gutenberg's settlement of his debt to Fust? Or had they been Fust's property all along? The types were valuable, but they were not the be-all and end-all of future printing. Fust and Schoeffer essentially set them aside, only bothering to print sundry editions of the Donatus with them while the team developed more versatile typefaces. Meanwhile, Gutenberg retained his improved DK types and a press or two, continued printing small fare for the next few years and appears to have suffered no permanent financial hardship or loss of social status. After working under Fust's profit-driven direction for several years, Gutenberg may have been fairly happy to part ways.

Fust wanted very much to continue printing books with Peter Schoeffer, but not with Gutenberg. He was taking a major

risk: allowing Gutenberg to take his knowledge elsewhere raised
the immediate possibility of a competing printing shop in Mainz.
But here one might do well to consider Fust's managerial point
of view: a modern-day employer might have described Gutenberg
as a valuable colleague who achieves good results under pressure,
albeit one who does so only after stretching deadlines and causing unnecessary emotional stress; one who can solve problems
independently but has trouble working as a team member; whose
communication skills, organization and time management need
improvement; whose sense of superiority and impatience with
colleagues (including those in positions of authority) undermines
the team as a whole; whose shortfall of agreed-upon goals,
despite working overtime, raises the suggestion that he may be
diverting company time or even assets to personal or outside
projects. Such a person would be difficult to keep as a partner
in the long run.

For all of its revelations, the Helmasperger Instrument presents an incomplete picture. It speaks of Fust's money and his
disputed terms, but in no way excludes the possibility of other
investors. Did Jakob Fust want no part of his brother's venture?
Did Heinrich Gunther of St Christopher's and other churchmen play no role? What about Fust's other witnesses? Did the
future master printers Peter Schoeffer, Heinrich Keffer and
Bechtolff Ruppel von Hanau, all mentioned in the same document, have nothing of their own to invest? Were Gutenberg's
future associates, Dr Humery and the brothers Bechtermünze
(or the printers Mentelin, Eggestein or Zel), involved at this
early stage? Three decades later, Abbot Tritheim recounted
Schoeffer's recollection that 4,000 florins had been expended
before the completion of the Bible's third quire – far more than
Fust's documented input. This figure is often taken to be an
exaggeration, but even so, when compared to the disputed sums
cited in the Helmasperger Instrument, all coming from Fust

alone, it puts the total expenditures for the Bible on a different order of magnitude. It is possible that Gutenberg had pulled together thousands of florins from various sources, and it just so happens that the one document that has survived concerns only Fust's settlement.

Three salient facts regarding Gutenberg's role in the development of printing emerge from the Helmasperger Instrument: first, he had been engaged with Fust in the production of books in Mainz for perhaps five years leading up to 1455; second, whereas Gutenberg had worked on minor projects independent of Fust during this period, the immensely expensive joint project can have been none other than the 42-line Bible, one of the most beautiful books ever printed; and third, Gutenberg had developed the printing apparatus himself and oversaw the daily labour and expenditures while Fust supplied necessary funds to bring the project to a profitable realization. Whereas many rich men of the time might have fulfilled Fust's financial role, and the calligrapher Peter Schoeffer doubtless contributed important improvements to the new types and printing process, it seems altogether fitting that Gutenberg ended up with his name – and his name alone – attached to history's most famous book.

The first printed Bible quickly exerted widespread impact across Germany. Subsequent editions that used it as copytext were printed in Strasbourg (c. 1460), Bamberg (c. 1461) and Mainz (1462), and another ninety editions appeared before the end of the century, most tracing their texts through two or three generations back to the first edition. Its influence continued in a slightly different way about a dozen years after its completion, when another Bible project was in the works in Mainz. This was a giant two-volume Latin Bible financed circa 1466–9 by Volpert von Ders (d. 1478), former master of the cathedral school, now chamberlain of the cathedral and apostolic protonotary (illus. 30). The existence of this Bible should give

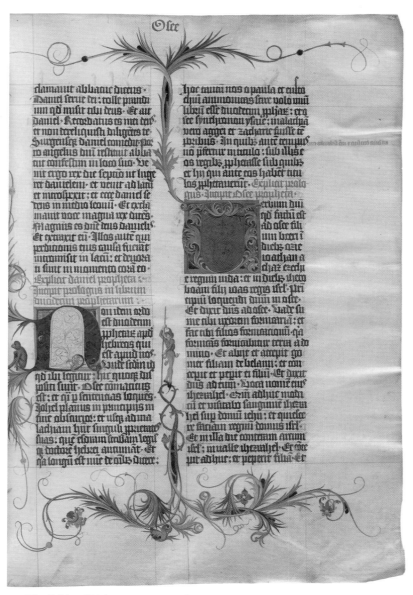

30 The Bible of Volpert von Ders, illuminated manuscript, Mainz region, c. 1458, first leaf of the Minor Prophets.

pause to all who might assert that Gutenberg's new typographic method transformed the calculus of European book production once and for all. Volpert's Bible is a manuscript, written out by hand in a *textus quadratus* script that is exceedingly large and wasteful of precious vellum, perhaps by the same faithful penman who had written out the 'Giant Bible' for Rudolf von Rüdesheim some fifteen years earlier. Moreover, it was illuminated by several artisans, one of whom, known today as the 'Fust Master', had illuminated the 42-line Bibles now in the Morgan Library and the Biblioteca Nacional in Madrid. Volpert's scribe and illuminators were called upon to provide a degree of grandeur and luxury that the printed Bibles could not. However, they depended on the printers in one important, perhaps startling respect: here the Latin text, carefully written out in columns of 36 lines, was copied directly and exclusively from the specific readings, variants and prologues printed in the 42-line Bible – Volpert's magnificent manuscript was, in essence, a 'Gutenberg Bible' that was copied out by hand.

While the 'work of the books' in Mainz would revolutionize how European books were made, this was by no means accomplished overnight. Long after Gutenberg's lifetime, professional scribes continued to earn important commissions, luxurious manuscripts fulfilled devotional and courtly functions that printed books could not, and people in need of all manner of books with limited or local appeal remained content to produce them one at a time. But when it came to making a particular text more widely available quickly, whether for the sake of societal impact or for mere profit, the miraculous men in Mainz now had the means to outproduce all of the scribes at once.

FIVE

The Wonderful Concord

No printer wants to see his pressmen sit idle. But not every printing job can be a Church-financed indulgence campaign, or such a colossal venture as the Latin Bible. Ephemera and day jobs must fill the spaces in the working schedule between large projects: at the end of the day, printing something costs less than printing nothing. Gutenberg realized this early on and set to work with the DK types to print numerous editions of the Donatus and other bread-and-butter projects. One of these, probably printed in 1456 or 1457, was a small broadside that provides its own title: *Cisianus zu dutsche*. A mnemonic guide to the Christian calendar, the *Cisianus* took its name from the first syllables of the original Latin verses: *Cisio* is short for the Circumcision of Christ on 1 January, while *Janus* indicates the first month of the year. Its usefulness resided in the fact that fifteenth-century Germans generally did not record dates as numbered days of the month, but by referring to the nearest saint's day or holiday. The information was organized into three rhyming couplets per month, and, as the German heading explained, 'each word provides the day.' Thus, in February, labelled *Hornung* in the left column, the verse itself does not make much sense, but what is important is that the fourteenth word is *Valentinus*. Similarly, the month of May begins *Meye das Crutze hat funden Johannes* ('May, the Cross hath found John'). The point was not that St John found any such thing, but rather that the Feast of

31 *Cisianus zu dutsche* (Mainz: DK types, c. 1456).

the Holy Cross fell on the third day of the month, while St John's feast day was the sixth of May. Naturally, the word for Christmas (*Wynacht*) appears in the very last line as the 25th word in the December sequence. Although the dialect rings of Strasbourg, the interpolations of St Margaret (13 July), St Arbogast (20 July),

St Willibrord (7 November) and the obscure St Bilhildis, founder of Kloster Altmünster in Mainz (27 November), argue for use in and near Mainz (illus. 31).

Another publication of around 1456–7 was the *Provinciale Romanum*. This small ten-leaf booklet listed more than five hundred bishoprics of the Roman Church, arranged according to the provinces of their various archbishops: thus, Germany had

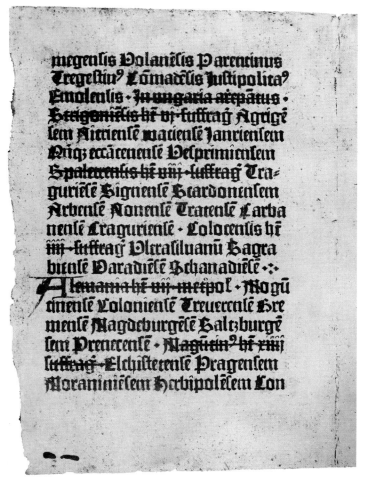

32 *Provinciale Romanum* (Mainz: DK types, *c.* 1456), last seen in 1937.

seven metropolitan sees – Mainz, Cologne, Trier, Bremen, Magdeburg, Salzburg and Brixen – after which were listed all fourteen of the suffragan bishoprics belonging to Mainz, the five belonging to Cologne and so on (the see of Antioch was stated to have 154 bishoprics, but they were not listed).[1] The booklet seems not to have been produced for any particular occasion, and would have been a useful reference only for a limited number of inexperienced clerics. Nevertheless, it was considered worth printing.

Other printings were more timely. Shortly after Pope Nicholas v died in March 1455 (a few weeks prior to the conclusion of the Cyprus indulgence campaign), his successor, the aged Spanish Cardinal Alfonso de Borgia, took the name of Callixtus III and made a special vow to defend Christianity against the Ottoman advances in the Mediterranean and Balkans, with the ultimate goal of retaking Jerusalem. In June 1456 he promulgated a viciously anti-Islamic bull calling for support from the homefront in the form of prayers to be said at the midday ringing of church bells throughout Christendom.[2] By then a spectacular comet, later known as Halley's, was visible in the evening sky. Alarm increased when news arrived that a huge army led by Sultan Mehmed II, conqueror of Constantinople, was laying siege to the Serbian stronghold at Belgrade on the Danube. However, on 22 July 1456, seemingly as an answer to the bell-ringing and prayers, János Hunyadi broke the siege with a stunning counter-attack that effectively ended the sultan's westward campaign. To this day, the noon *angelus* commemorating this victory rings from many church belfries. Back in Mainz, Archbishop Dietrich von Erbach approved the announcement of the papal bull throughout his archdiocese, and Hermann Rosenberg, canon of Mainz Cathedral, ordered this to be done on 26 October 1456. Manuscript copies were written out, but of course now there was another way: Gutenberg and his helpers used the DK types to print a twelve-leaf pamphlet of the Latin text under the title *Bulla thurcorum* (illus. 33) and a fourteen-leaf German translation, *Die Bulla widder die Turcken*, for the townspeople to hear. Fust and Schoeffer (as far as the lack of copies suggests) were either not ready to print the *Bulla* that winter or had no interest in it; only single copies of the two DK-type pamphlets survive, both dated '1456' by hand, and both discovered centuries later in Erfurt. The booklets do not appear to have been officially overseen by authorities in Mainz Cathedral; the Latin text reveals several corruptions that had to be corrected with marginal annotations by their owners.

Towards the very end of 1456 Gutenberg created Europe's first known printing of a purely medical text: a wall-chart titled *Conjunctiones et oppositiones solis et lune*. This Latin 'blood-letting calendar' identified the planetary conjunctions or oppositions in the visible sky that physicians would use during the coming year of 1457 to determine the astrologically propitious days for therapeutic phlebotomies and purgatives. For a one-year period the broadside offered three lines of monthly life-saving medical advice, after which it became a virtually useless sheet of paper. As the unique fragment found in Mainz (and now in Paris) was a random survival, and as there was nothing special (medically speaking) about the year 1457, it is probable that Gutenberg printed such sheets annually for local use over the course of his career.[3]

Yet another paper broadside that Gutenberg printed circa 1457 was the *Respice domine*, a short Latin prayer that expressed abject gratitude to merciful God for sacrificing his son for the sake of humanity. Excerpted from the *Meditationes* of the twelfth-century Benedictine abbot Eckbert of Schönau, the brother of St Elizabeth of Schönau, the text also appeared in several contemporary manuscripts, including one now in the municipal library in Mainz, and during the 1480s and '90s the Parisian printer

alixtus eps̄ ſeru⁹ ſeruoꝛ dei
venēabilib⁹ fr̄ib⁹ p̄ſiarchis
arc̄p̄is epis electis neccn̄ō dilectis
filiis eoꝛ in ſpūalibus vicariis ac
abbatib⁹ rectc̄iſqȝ eccāſticis p̄ſonis
vbilibet p orbē x̄p̄ianū cōſtitutis
Salutē ꝛ apſicā bn̄dictionē Cum
hiis ſupiorib⁹ annis impius nois̄
x̄p̄iani pſecutor Thurccoꝛ tyrān⁹
p⁹ oppreſſā cōſtātinopoli ciuitatē
in qua omē gen⁹ crudelitatis exer-
cuit ſeuiēs nō ſolū ſed ex quo i deū
nr̄m nō poterat in ſuos ſc̄oꝛ qȝ reli
quias impii deſiderii conatū totū
virib⁹ ſit pſecut⁹ fideles p̄ll̄ ad q̄
valuit aſpirare aſſiduis cladibus
affligēdo ita vt noue plage i dies
calamitates nūdent̄ Cūqȝ eciā q̄

33 Callixtus III, *Bulla thurcorum* (Mainz: DK types, 1456).

Antoine Vérard included an extended version of the text as an auxiliary prayer in several Books of Hours.[4] In the sixteenth century the prayer appeared with further modifications in versions attributed to various writers. Nothing seems to have occasioned the first printing of the prayer other than its popularity.

Around 1458 Gutenberg upgraded his operation with a very sharp recasting of the DK types. He used the new 'third state' of this typeface for the first time in an impressive edition of German *Ephemerides* broadsides, now known as the 'Astronomical Calendars' or 'Planetary Tables', with each broadside printed on the front sides of six sheets of vellum. These were pasted together to form single oblong placards, each nearly a yard wide, that were suitable for hanging on a wall. Centuries later, all but one of the 'Astronomical Calendars' had been lost, and when that unique survivor (illus. 34) was rediscovered at Wiesbaden in 1901, only two of its six sheets had survived – the ones bearing the text for January through April (during the Second World War, these too were lost). The fact that the table's positioning of the Moon, Mercury, Venus, Mars, Jupiter and Saturn among the constellations during January through April corresponded to the sky as it appeared in 1448 initially misled modern scholars to believe that it dated from that year, or perhaps 1447. However, closer analysis showed that the calendar's functionality was not limited to any particular year, but rather was able to serve over a longer period as a general reference for astrological forecasting of horoscopes of a somewhat homespun variety.[5]

The survival of this array of booklets and broadsides, as well as several editions of the Donatus, shows that Gutenberg made fairly constant use of the DK types during his first decade back in Mainz, if only for inexpensive works of transient nature. However, at this point, around 1458, Gutenberg had a much more ambitious, if not quite viable, project on his mind. A trio of battered paper fragments discovered in 1948 in a forgotten

34 Fragments of the *Astronomical Calendar* (Mainz: DK types, c. 1458), lost during the Second World War.

binding at the Jagiellonian University Library in Kraków, printed with the third state of the DK types, turned out to consist of trial sheets for the *Astronomical Calendar*, yet another Donatus grammar and, amazingly, a large folio Latin Bible (Inc. 2267). These trials were hastily printed on the recycled leaves of an account book compiled for a cloth merchant in Mainz during the 1390s – possibly preserving the trade activities of one of Gutenberg's relatives, if not those of his father, Friele. The fragment of the Latin Bible, cut down but easily extrapolated from the lines expended on the text of Genesis, would have consisted of double columns of forty lines. This of course was the same number of lines with which Gutenberg, Fust and company had initiated the edition that became the 42-line Bible. But columns of forty lines of the larger DK types would measure more than 2 inches taller than those of the 42-line Bible, making the Bible of the Kraków trial sheet a far larger and longer book. Indeed, its paper cannot have been Royal folio, but rather the largest and most expensive of all available paper sizes: Imperial folio. This new Bible venture, seemingly as impractical as it was grandiose, was doomed to an early demise. Gutenberg's realization that such an edition was beyond his reach may have coincided with his seemingly abrupt decision to give up on the DK types altogether; no further printed specimens from Mainz are known. But the idea of such a handsome Bible was not long forgotten.

Obviously Gutenberg was not ruined by the settlement of the 'work of the books' in 1455. But it is undeniable that the functionality of Gutenberg's printing operation in the years following the completion of the 42-line Bible never rose above the level of making ends meet. He had not dreamed all those years ago of merely dotting the narrow streets of Mainz with ephemeral broadsides, pamphlets and the occasional Donatus. But now, without the backing of wealthy investors, such ambitious folio book projects – theology, liturgies, law codes or any of the other important book genres – seemed out of the question or doomed to fail. His situation presented a stark contrast to what was happening in Fust and Schoeffer's new printing shop in a nearby neighbourhood in Mainz. There, on 14 August 1457, one of the most beautiful and luxurious books ever printed was brought to completion: a Royal folio *Psalterium cum canticis*, containing the 150 Latin psalms and accompanying canticles and hymns for liturgical use. Printed exclusively on vellum with two very large *textus quadratus* typefaces that rank among the most beautiful ever made, the *Psalter* is adorned throughout with red-printed rubrics, hundreds of red or blue capitals and numerous very large, variously sized decorative initials that were printed in red and blue with pairs of interlocking plates in imitation of the calligraphic infill and marginal flourishes of expert hand-decoration. Perhaps because the press run of the *Psalter* was much smaller than that of the Bible, the reservations that had put an end to the printing of the Bible's red rubrics were long gone. The multicoloured initials, requiring more complex press-work than anything previously envisioned, represented a major selling point: they rendered the text complete.

The contents of the first printed *Psalter* were closely super-vised by priestly advisors, who must have instructed the printers on what sorts of letters, rubrics, abbreviations and ornaments would be required for this essential liturgical book. While the larger types were designed to convey the texts of the psalms and canticles for recitation during the Divine Office, the smaller types provided the antiphon texts that were to be sung in the choir; blank spaces were left for musical notation to be added by hand above the printed verses. In a concession to the needs of particular communities of worship, the *Psalter* was available in two distinct issues: a longer 175-leaf issue, intended specifically for use within the archdiocese of Mainz, which was augmented with 32 extra leaves containing 81 additional hymns and the

Inuitat· Dominū deum nostrū, Venite adremus

Ps Venite exul· asi Quia mirabilia· Evovae, ps

Cantate domio canticū nouū:
quia mirabilia fecit, Salua-
bit sibi dextera eius: et brachiū
sanctum eius, Notū fecit dūs
salutare suum: in conspectu gentiū reuela-
uit iusticiam suam, Recordatus est mise-
ricordie sue: et veritatis sue domui israhel,
Viderūt omnes termini terre: salutare dei
nostri, Iubilate domio omnis terra: cantate et exultate et psallite, Psallite domio
in cythara in cythara et voce psalmi: in tu-
bis ductilibus et voce tube cornee, Iubilate in cōspectu regis dūi: moueat mare z
plenitudo eius: orbis terraz et qui habitāt
in eo, Flumina plaudēt manu simsl mon-
tes exultabunt a conspectu dūi: quū venit

35 *Psalterium cum canticis* (Mainz: Johann Fust and Peter Schoeffer,
14 August 1457).

Vigils of the Dead; and a shorter 143-leaf issue, intended for universal ecclesiastical or monastic use, which therefore lacked the final three quires and left blank spaces for different antiphons to be written in by the eventual monastic users in accordance with their local traditions.

A stunning technical triumph, the Mainz *Psalter* is a testament to the ingenuity and artistry of its printers as well as the qualitative ambitions of its designers. Few printing houses would ever again attempt such fiercely difficult typographic operations, and even fewer would achieve such an effective balance between function and beauty. A sense of great accomplishment is expressed in the book's colophon, which established the *Psalter* as both the earliest European printed book to bear the date of its completion and the first to credit its producers by name (in translation):

> The present book of the Psalms, adorned with the beauty of capital letters and sufficiently marked with rubrics, has been fashioned by the artful invention of printing by means of letter forms made without the driving of the pen; and in praise of God it has been brought faithfully and industriously to completion by Johann Fust, citizen of Mainz, and Peter Schoeffer of Gernsheim, in the year of the Lord one thousand cccc lvii [1457], on the vigil of the Feast of the Assumption [14 August].[6]

Johann Fust had taken all that he had learned (and earned) from the 'work of the books' and transformed it into a printing factory of seemingly unlimited potential. He promoted young Peter Schoeffer, making him into a kind of artistic and technical director of the press, asking him once again to produce even more beautiful typefaces and to develop an ingenious system for printing decorative initials in multiple colours. It is possible that these initials had been envisioned from Gutenberg's very first discussions of typography, but only now did they make their first appearance. This time, having attained success with the risky Bible, Fust did not yield to the fearful impracticality and expense of the work, and he was rewarded with glorious results. Fust had provided all that was needed to make sure that the *Psalter* became the virtually perfect, quite heavenly printed book that three or four years earlier could only have been dreamed about. But the team of Fust and Schoeffer did not stop there. They also completed impressive folio editions of the *Canon missae* (c. 1458) for insertion within old manuscript missals, the immense *Psalterium Benedictinum* (29 August 1459) and Guillelmus Durandus' *Rationale divinorum officiorum* (6 October 1459), the first book printed with a much smaller rotunda type for extended reading, and the first to be marketed successfully in Italy. Each of these, like the first *Psalter*, was adorned with red and blue printed initials. Next to come from their press was the very large folio *Constitutiones* of Pope Clement v (25 June 1460), devoid of large two-coloured initials yet very handsome, which was both the first printing of Christian canon law and the first text to be printed with a surrounding commentary in smaller types. The Durandus, the Benedictine Psalter and the Clementine *Constitutiones* likewise bore celebratory colophons that expressed Fust and Schoeffer's pride in their achievements, yet none of them mentioned the former colleague whose earlier achievements had shown them the way.

By 1460 the cradle and capital of European typography had surrendered its monopoly. In that year Johann Mentelin, a scribe and episcopal notary in Strasbourg, completed the printing of a one-volume folio in that city (illus. 36), which was nothing less than the Latin Bible. Indeed, in 1474 an Italian chronicler recalled that Mentelin had been printing three hundred sheets per day as early as 1458. Unfortunately, modern historians cannot be certain how or from whom Mentelin learned to print. But

36 *Biblia latina* (Strasbourg: Johann Mentelin, not after 1460).

there are really only two or three candidates for the distinction of training Mentelin, and only one of them, Gutenberg,
had a known connection with Strasbourg, while the other two
must be seen as Mentelin's most direct competitors. Moreover,
Mentelin's editions do not share the opulence or beauty of the
books from Fust and Schoeffer's press. His Latin Bible bespeaks
economy. It was printed exclusively on paper, not vellum, using
a compact Gothic rotunda type that reduced the length of the

text to 427 folio leaves, as opposed to the 641 leaves required of the larger-type 42-line Bible. Mentelin's mainly ecclesiastical buyers tended not to have their Bibles adorned with lavish illumination, prefering utilitarian rubrication in red and blue. The market for his Strasbourg edition was mainly the upper Rhineland (to the south of Mainz) and Switzerland, as well as several destinations to the east along the Danube River, across Bavaria and as far as Salzburg. After a hiatus of nearly three years, during which Mentelin appears to have printed only one indulgence, he printed his second major book, a folio edition of the all-important 'Second part of Part Two' of St Thomas Aquinas' massive *Summa theologica*, in which he introduced a new, smaller rotunda type (his first Bible types were never seen again). Then in 1466, after another three-year hiatus, he produced three books, including the first edition of a vernacular Bible in High German. Strasbourg would become a chief rival to Mainz in the second decade of European printing.

Around the same time that Mentelin set up his printing shop in Strasbourg, that is, around 1458, Gutenberg seems to have relinquished the tools necessary for casting a final state of the DK types to some well-trained printers in the cathedral town of Bamberg, some 190 kilometres (120 mi.) to the east of Mainz. Whether or not he also ventured to Bamberg to show the way, by 1460 these printers, supported by Johann I von Schaumburg, Bishop of Bamberg, were giving shape to the inventor's dream of another large-type Latin Bible. Copied from the 42-line Mainz edition, but composed into columns of 36 lines of a recasting of Gutenberg's even larger DK types, these grand Bibles – requiring 884 leaves of paper or vellum – were sold throughout the diocese of Bamberg in 1461, while Bishop Schaumburg presented some copies to monasteries as diplomatic gifts (illus. 37).

In Mainz, meanwhile, Fust and Schoeffer were busy producing their own two-volume Latin Bible, a crowning achievement

of Europe's pioneering decade of printing (illus. 38). The first
Bible to bear the names of its printers, its place of printing
and its date of completion (14 August 1462), this fourth edition featured the small Gothic rotunda typeface that was first
used in the colophon of the 1459 *Durandus*. Although it dis-
pensed with the large two-coloured initials that had adorned
the Mainz *Psalters*, the Bible did include red rubrics, occasional
red or blue chapter initials, and Fust and Schoeffer's armorial
device at the end of each volume (illus. 39). Unlike the other
editions, this Bible was truly a pan-European success, as many
copies were exported to France, Italy and other distant markets,
making it the most 'international' edition of the early period of
European typography. Moreover, it proved to be a much more
enduring Bible than the earlier editions in that its usefulness
(and identifiability) transcended the Reformation, as scholars
remained aware of its value through the sixteenth and seventeenth centuries. Already in 1549, by which time no one could
remember anything useful about the 42-line Bible, Conrad
Gesner, the 'father of modern bibliography', listed the Bible of
1462 first in chronological order under the heading for the Latin
Bibles in his *Partitiones theologicae, Pandectarum universalium*
(Zurich, 1549). Indeed, as a signed and dated Bible, Fust and
Schoeffer's edition never had to be rescued from historical oblivion. Although Gutenberg had nothing to do with its production,
the Bible of 1462 was the first book to realize the inventor's
highest aspirations for the widespread, long-term use of beautiful
printed books.

  Three further titles were printed in Mainz in the period
around 1460, not by Fust and Schoeffer, but anonymously, with
a new, very small Gothic rotunda text type. One of these was
Aquinas' *De articulis fidei et ecclesiae sacramentis*, a short treatise
on the Christian articles of faith and the holy sacraments as
enforcements against heresies, which was required reading for all

Explicit epla scda Ad corinthios
Incipit prologus in eplam beati pauli

Galathe ad galathas. sunt greci. Hii ubu ueritatis primu ab aplo acceperut: sed post discessum eius temptati sut a falsis aplis: ut in lege i circucisione ut uertereur. Hos apostolus reuocat ad side ueritatis: scribes eis ab ephese. Explicit prologus Incipit Ad galathas. ca

Paulus apostolus no ab hominibus neq per homine sed p ihm cristum et deu patrem q suscitauit eu a mortuis: et q mecu sunt omes fres: ecclesijs galathie. Gratia uobis et pax a deo pre nro et duo ihesu cristo: q tradit semetipm p pctis nris ut eriperet nos de presenti seculo neq secdm uoluntate dei et pris nri: cui est gloria in secula seculorum ame. Miror q sic tam cito trasseremini ab eo qui uos uocauit in gratia cristi in aliud euangeliu qd no est aliud: nisi sunt aliqui q uos coturbant: et uolut couertere euageliu cristi. Sed licet nos aut agelus de celo euagelizet uobis preterq qd euagelizauimus uobis: anathema sit. Sicut pdiximus et nunc

iterum dico: si qs uobis euagelizauerit preter id qd accepistis: anathema sit. Modo em hominib; suadeo an deo: An qro homnib; place: Si adhuc hominib; placere xpi seru no essem. Notu em uobis facio fres euageliu qd euagelizatu est a me: qa no e secdm hoiem. Neq em ego ab hoie accepi illud neq; didici: sed p reuelatione ihu cristi. Audistis em couersatione mea aliquado in iudaismo: qm supra modu psequebar ecclesia dei i repugnaba illa: et proficieba i iudaismo supra multos coetaneos meos in genere meo: abudatius emulator existes paternar mear traditionu. Cu aut placuit ei q me segregauit de utero matris mee et uocauit p gratia suam ut reuelaret filiu suu in me ut euagelizare illu in getibus: cotinuo no acquieui carni i saguini. Neq; ueni iherosolima ad atecessores meos apostolos sed abij in arabia: i iterum reuersus sum damasci. Deinde post anos tres ueni iherosolima uidere petru: et mansi apud eu diebus quindecim. Aliu aut aplorum uidi nemine: nisi iacobu fratre dui. Que aut scribo uobis: ecce cora deo quia no mentior. Deinde ueni in partes syrie et cilicie. Eram aut ignotus facie ecclesijs

37 The 36-line Bible (Bamberg: Albrecht Pfister, not after 1461).

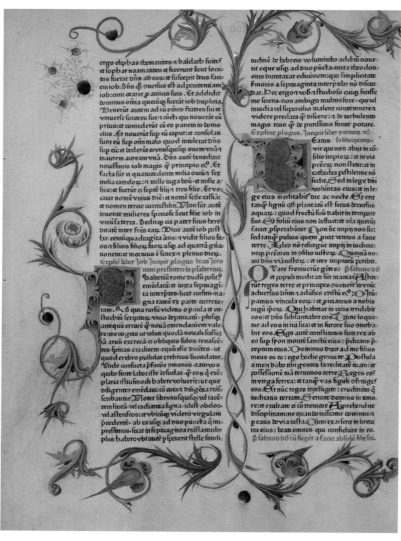

38 *Biblia latina* (Mainz: Johann Fust and Peter Schoeffer, 14 August 1462), psalms.

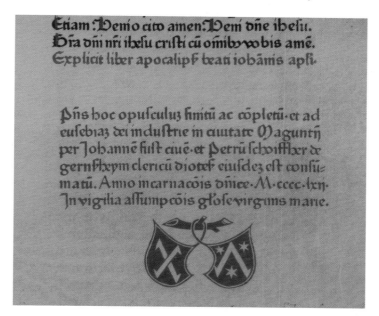

39 *Biblia latina* (Mainz: Johann Fust and Peter Schoeffer, 14 August 1462), colophon in vol. II.

priests within the archdiocese of Mainz. The other was Matthaeus de Cracovia's *Dialogus rationis et conscientiae de frequenti usu communionis* (illus. 40), a somewhat longer tract on the benefits of attending Mass, that took the form of a dialogue between Conscience, who laments mankind's sinfulness, and Reason, who trusts in God's redemptive mercy. The short Aquinas text was printed twice, once on 12 leaves bearing 36 lines per page, and once on 13 leaves with only 34 lines per page. Strangely, although the number of lines and their alignment differed in the two printings, the locations of each and every individual letter remained rigidly the same. Clearly these two versions were made from the same setting of type, but this was rearranged so that each page relegated two more lines of text to the subsequent page. Likewise, the Matthaeus de Cracovia quarto was printed in two virtually identical versions, once on the same paper that is found

ultoꝛ tam clericoꝛ q̃ laicoꝛ quere
la ē non modica. occupacio grauis
et questio dubiosa. quomodo quis
se habere debeat in celebrando uel
cōmunicando Quando uidelicet ac
cedere. Quomodo accedentes moti
uel dispositi esse. Aut quibus motiuis uł indispo
sicionibus abstinere debeant Et an melius sit con
tinue sumere corpus xp̃i. Frequenter. aut raro. De
tam utili et multis quodāmodo necessaria materia
sepe interrogans. pluries interrogatus. audiui ua
ria et uidi. Nec tñ adhuc sic quietus sum quin se
pe disceptem et litigem in me ip̃o Jam uolo acce
dere Jam nolo. hinc attrahoꝛ. illinc retrahoꝛ. nūc
spe diuine misicoꝛdie animoꝛ ut faciam. nunc ti
more misere consciencie aut districti iudicii retre
oꝛ ut dimittam. Et ita nescio quid deo magꞇ pla
ceat. quid m̃ magis expediat Vereoꝛ me sepius
accedere dñ abstinendū est. et dñ accedendū est o
mittere. ymmo q̃ꝗ tamdiu disputando mecum
dubito ꝙ ex ipa disputacōne tempus transit uel
alias impedimentū occurrit et negligo Licet autē
hijs dubijs et tot ambiguitatibus conscienciaꝝ
satisfacere nō ualeam et hec lis nō nūꝗ ualde bo
na sit. ꝗ ex ea consurgit discussio consciencie ut
ꝓbet homo seip̃m. ꝗ tamen consciencia q̃ꝗ er
ronea uel nimis scrupulosa est. et ad unam ꝑtem
tali motiuo mouetur quo uel ad oppositam ꝑtē
uel nichil omnino moueri deberet. Jdcirco uisum
est michi iudicet qui uoluerit an bene. ꝙ non ē

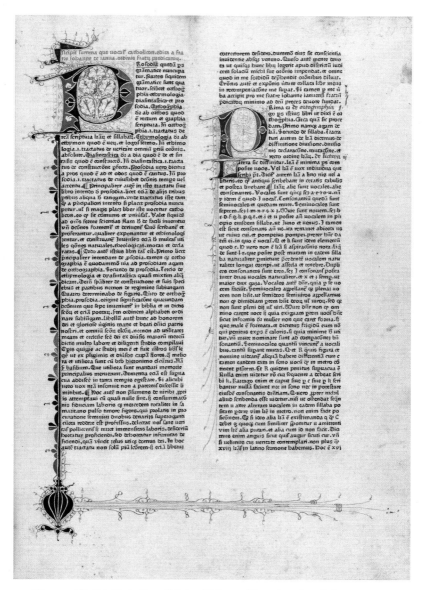

41 Giovanni Balbi, *Catholicon* (Mainz: [Johann Gutenberg], 1460).

in the 36-line Aquinas, and once on the paper of the 34-line Aquinas, albeit with what appears to be typographic damage or interference to multiple lines of text on f. 20 verso throughout the print run. A copy of the former issue, long preserved in Paris, ends with a contemporary inscription to the effect that 'Heynricus Keppfer de Moguncia' had loaned the booklet to its unnamed owner but never reclaimed it.[7] This book lender in Mainz was doubtless the same 'Heinrich Keffer' who had been listed as one of Gutenberg's workmen in the Helmasperger Instrument in 1455.

By far the most significant book to emerge from this anonymous Mainz press was the first printed edition of the *Catholicon*, a Royal folio of 373 leaves (illus. 41). This essential dictionary of medieval Latin, completed in 1286 by the Dominican friar Giovanni Balbi (d. 1298) of Genoa, consists of four treatises on Latin grammar and syntax and an alphabetical vocabulary with entries for some 15,000 Latin words (including *honorifica-bilitudinitatibus*) and their definitions, etymologies, derivations and paradigms for all declensions and conjugations. Always in demand, the *Catholicon* was guaranteed to sell: in Augsburg the scribe Heinrich Lengfeldt had finished copying one massive manuscript of the text in 1458 and soon undertook another that he would complete in 1462.[8] The first printed edition ends with a versified Latin colophon that identifies Mainz as the place of printing (thereby becoming the first European book to do so explicitly) and 1460 as the year of its completion. The colophon's verses express pride in German ingenuity but remain silent regarding the identity of the book's printer. Clearly, the *Catholicon* was not printed by Fust and Schoeffer, who virtually always publicized their names and printing achievements in exultant red-letter colophons. Moreover, the small Gothic rotunda book-hand of the *Catholicon*, reminiscent of the types of the 31-line Cyprus indulgence, would have been entirely superfluous in their shop, which already had the more calligraphic 'Durandus' types for printing non-liturgical texts. Whoever was responsible for the 1460 Mainz *Catholicon* – and there can be very few candidates – left evidence of an entirely different personality, character and outlook. There is something poignant and admirable in the fact that the printer was content to remain anonymous, even after completing such an enormous task. In place of self-praise, his colophon expressed a devout thankfulness for the recently granted ability to produce such a book, not with ancient writing implements, but with wondrous new tools (*mira patronarum formarum que concordia proporcione et modulo*):

> With the help of the Most High, through whose volition
> children become eloquent, and who often 'has hid these
> things from the wise and prudent, and has revealed
> them unto babes' [Matthew 11:25], this noble book, the
> Catholicon, has been printed and completed as the years
> of the Lord's incarnation number MCCCCLX [1460], in the
> city of Mainz within the great German nation – which
> God in his clemency has provided with higher illumination
> of the mind and thus favoured above all other nations –
> without the use of a reed, a stylus or a pen, but rather by
> the wonderful concord, proportion and measure of patrices
> [punches?] and formes [pieces cast in a mould?]. Now let
> praise and glory be rendered to the Holy Father, the Son,
> and the Holy Spirit, with endless praise to Mary. Thanks
> be to God.

It will be recalled that when the Sorbonne professor Guillaume Fichet wrote in 1471 of the spread of printers beyond the walls of Mainz, he identified Gutenberg as the first to conceive of the new art, but made no mention of specific printed books. However, Fichet's comparison of Gutenberg's invention to the older methods of writing with reeds or quills directly paraphrased the colophon of the Mainz *Catholicon*. This fact is quite suggestive. Printed books bearing the names of Fust and Schoeffer may have been seen in France as early as 1457, but when Fichet sought to expound upon this newly invented art of making books, he did not think of Fust or Schoeffer. The first name that came to his mind was Gutenberg's, and the words that he selected to explain the novel nature of this unfamiliar art came directly from the Mainz *Catholicon*. Fichet's focus on Gutenberg and (of all books) the *Catholicon* not only shows that he considered Gutenberg to be the inventor of printing; it strongly suggests that he believed, or knew, that the anonymous printer of that book was none other than Gutenberg.

We last left Gutenberg in his workshop in Mainz, aged about sixty, finishing off the last of the ephemeral booklets and broadsides he printed with his old DK types and deciding at long last that those large *textus quadrata* types were no longer the key to his future. He seems neither to have retained the old DK typeface, which he may have melted down to provide material for other projects, nor to have kept the means to reproduce it; in any event, no trace of it survives from Mainz after 1458, at which point its final casting began to serve the printers of the 36-line Bible in Bamberg. However, Gutenberg is known to have left behind substantial materials for printing (*truckwerk*) when he died in 1468. According to a still-extant letter of 26 February 1468, Conrad Humery, doctor of canon law and former chancellor of the city council in Mainz, had promised the Archbishop of Mainz that the 'numerous formes, letters, instruments, tools, and other items pertaining to the work of printing' that Johann Gutenberg had left when he died, and which remained Humery's property, would be used exclusively for printing within Mainz, and further, that these properties would not be sold to anyone who was not a citizen of Mainz, even at an increased price (one wonders what Peter Schoeffer of Gernsheim, not a citizen of

Mainz, thought of this stipulation). Thus, although Gutenberg stopped using his DK types around 1458, until 1468 he still owned printing materials that were considered valuable and worthy of retention within the city. This almost certainly was not some forgotten, unused typeface, but rather the new material made for the printing of the *Catholicon* in 1460. Indeed, a passel of lecture notes on canon law compiled by Conrad Humery at the University of Bologna in 1430, long preserved in the Vatican Library, was bound in a wrapper made from a paper leaf from none other than the Mainz *Catholicon*. It bears no rubrication, and therefore appears to have been cut from an unused waste sheet. Given that the Vatican Library bindery has never, as a rule, gone out of its way to match up old printed scraps from Mainz with even older lecture notes from Mainz, this historical coupling of the *Catholicon* and the owner of Gutenberg's printing equipment in 1468 makes it nearly certain that Gutenberg did indeed print the *Catholicon*.

The Mainz *Catholicon* is quite unlike most fifteenth-century printed books. Close examination shows that the surviving copies were published in four distinct issues, that is, each copy was printed on one of three separate paper supplies, or on vellum. Each of these issues clearly derives from the same setting of type: excepting some variable horizontal alignment affecting pairs of lines (but never singletons), the relative locations of each and every letter remain rigidly the same across every copy. Yet the division of virtually identical printings into separate paper varieties presents a real oddity, and a puzzle. One issue, with a two-line rubric printed in red on the first leaf, was printed on vellum. An identical issue was printed on paper bearing bull's head watermarks, the same paper that is found in Mentelin's Strasbourg edition of the Bible, which was available for sale in 1460. Another issue without the printed rubric was impressed with slightly less clarity on paper bearing the Gothic

'C' (Caselle?) watermarks of the Galliziani family paper mills in Basel, while yet another issue without the rubric was printed with less clarity on paper with 'tower' or 'crown' watermarks, evidently imported from Épinal, southwest of Strasbourg. What is truly surprising is that of these three paper supplies, only the bull's head paper is known to have been available at the end of the 1450s, and so could align with the date 'm.cccc.lx' that appears in the identical colophons of all four issues. A blank leaf bound in the copy of the bull's head paper *Catholicon* in Gotha bears an early inscription stating that the book was purchased in 1465 for the Augustinians at Altenburg by Otto Grisz, provost there from 1452 to 1468. By contrast, the Galliziani paper only became available for use in other datable books around 1469, while the tower or crown papers were first used around 1473, by which time Gutenberg was long dead.

Clearly, regardless of the '1460' in the colophon of the *Catholicon*, Gutenberg (or anyone else) could not have printed

42 Giovanni Balbi, *Catholicon* (Mainz: [Printer of the 'Galliziani' issue, dated '1460' but *c.* 1469), with an upside-down pair of lines.

a book in 1460 on reams of paper that did not exist until a decade or so later, and no human could possibly reset the 373 leaves several years later with such accuracy, letter by letter, so that the second and third editions are not immediately distinguishable. Nor could these pages be left for years as standing type – tumultuous years, as it turned out – and then printed afresh. So how, and why, were these virtually identical issues reprinted on different papers at different times? The surprising solution to the conundrum was discovered in 1982 by Paul Needham, who observed that various printing accidents in the *Catholicon*, each particular to the copies printed on its own variety of paper, always affected consecutive *pairs of complete lines* – whether they were composed upside-down (illus. 42), out of order, shifted sideways or damaged – and none of the accidents resulted in misplaced individual pieces of type. Tellingly, if something ever appeared to be 'moveable', such as a textual variant at the top of the first column of the last page of the letter Z, then it was only moveable as two entire lines at a time, as if those paired lines had been permanently fused together. As Needham concluded, this is all because the *Catholicon* was not printed with moveable types, but with solid strips of metal, some 49,000 in number, each representing a pair of lines of this text. As best this forgotten printing method can be reconstructed, Gutenberg's compositors set the text as usual with a set of preparatory types, and after it had been proofed for accuracy, the columns were separated into 33 pairs of lines, each of which was impressed into a receptive medium such as clay or fine wet sand to create individual two-line casting moulds. Hot metal was poured into each of these moulds, creating permanent two-line metal strips (or slugs) for printing, storing away and subsequent reprinting.

This innovation allowed for the bull's head paper and vellum issues of the *Catholicon* to have been printed in 1460, just as was stated in the colophon and was implied by the usage date of that paper. It also allowed for the second issue on Galliziani paper to have been recomposed from the thousands of pairs of lines and reprinted circa 1469 and for this process to be repeated for the tower and crown paper issue of around 1473. True, this innovation required long storage of 49,000 two-line slugs, and it made the work of the original printer significantly more difficult: they had to compose the types for this lengthy work and then recast them as fused two-line slugs, which then had to be stored in the correct order for later use. But in the end, these extra steps made the work of the subsequent printers exponentially easier: they could recompose several hundred pages in a matter of days by placing their sequences of 66 two-line slugs in proper order. This required far less time, difficulty and risk than composing the tricky abbreviated Latin with millions of individual types afresh.

Thus Gutenberg's second major typographic invention was, ironically, non-moveable types. As in blockbooks, this method granted the ability to reprint books without the necessity of recomposing moveable types. But whereas blockbooks were severely limited in their capacity to convey substantial texts, slug-books like the *Catholicon* made reprinting of the lengthiest and most important of works quite feasible. However, unlike Gutenberg's first great invention, this 'wonderful concord' did not catch on with other printers or lead to rapid improvements. Aside from the *Catholicon*, only two other books, the slender quarto tracts by Aquinas and Matthaeus de Cracovia, were made with the new two-line slug method; the first issues of around 1459–60, and the second ones of circa 1469. In 1470, two years after Gutenberg's demise, both of those titles and the *Catholicon* itself were advertised on a broadsheet that listed some twenty printed books to be made available through agents of Peter Schoeffer (of all people) in other towns. It appears that Dr Humery had looked to the only printer remaining in Mainz to help liquidate his assets by means of these reprints. Eventually, either he, Schoeffer or some other buyer melted the slugs down for more fruitful purposes.

In 1461 Gutenberg used the moveable preparatory types of the *Catholicon* to produce an indulgence in support of the rebuilding of the Collegiate Church of St Cyriacus at Neuhausen. A famous pilgrimage site just outside the walls of Worms, the next major city up the Rhine from Mainz, Neuhausen was the home of the relics of St Cyriacus, one of the Fourteen Holy Helpers who enjoyed widespread veneration in medieval Germany. Unfortunately, in June 1460 the ancient church at Neuhausen had been burned to the ground by mercenaries serving the newly elected Archbishop of Mainz, Diether von Isenburg, in his battles against the territorial ambitions of Frederick I, Elector Palatine of the Rhine. This embarrassing catastrophe caused outrage on all sides, and on 29 December 1460 Pope Pius II, formerly provost in Worms, granted an indulgence promising spiritual benefits to those who contributed to the reconstruction of St Cyriacus. As with the Cyprus indulgences of 1454–5, this urgent campaign was considered too important and far-reaching to be entrusted to only one press: by October 1461 Gutenberg (we assume) had printed separate oblong indulgences for men or for women with the 'Catholicon' types, Fust and Schoeffer had printed a pair of issues with their 'Durandus' types, and Johann Mentelin in Strasbourg had been called upon to print editions with his Latin Bible types for folks further to the southwest in Germany and Switzerland. Of all of Europe's printers, only Albrecht Pfister in Bamberg, the purveyor of large Gothic types that were not of his own making, was unable to participate in this holy campaign.

One of the surviving Catholicon-press indulgences for St Cyriacus (illus. 43), now in the State Archive in Ludwigsburg, near Stuttgart, was issued at Mundelsheim (Württemberg) to a

Iᴜ otum fit vniūſis pūtes Lãs inſpecturis Q̃ quia dicta anna vogt̃n Schwãŋꝗ augusten dioc pro repacōne ecclie ſcti Cyriaci ſtubuſen et ad op9 fabrice ipſi9 intant̃u contribuit q̃ laborãs aput eãdẽ pro duodecim dieb9 diſponi poſſit. Jdcoꝗ particeps Jndulgenaꝗ in fauore dicte ecclie per ſeriſſn̄i d̃rī nn̄i pium papꝝ ſcd̄m conceſſaꝗ eſſe debebit videlicet q̃ eliꝗ poſſit confeſſorem ydoneuꝗ q̃ eam ab oib9 Sentenciꝗs excōicacōis et alijo cẽſuris in q̃s nodum incidiſſe declarata et denũdata ẽſt ſtecnon ab omiib9 crimib9 petis et delictis m̃qbuſcũꝗ caſibus eciam ſedi aplice reſuatis ſemel in vita abſolue ac ei ſalutare peſtencã miũnꝗe neeno plenariã remiſſionem oim petōꝝ ſuoꝝ ſemel in mortis articulo auce aplica impartiri et concede ac vota oia exceptis votis ad hm̃ia aplōꝝ pet̃ et pauli: tre ſctẽ. ac ſcti Jacobi in alia pietatis opera maxie pro fabica p̃dicta ꝫmutare poſſit et valeat: Sic tñ q̃ ſatiſfaciat ſi alicui p ea ſatiſfactio impendẽda ſit Et contemptrix ſedis aplice et libratis ſtat9 eccliaſtici nō fueit neꝗ ſit Et ſinigl̃ ſextis Feijos per annũ l̃ loco ſexte feie qñ abiunce in illa ieiunae tenet alio die in ſepriana ieiunet Et ſi impdicto anno vl̃ aliꝗ ei9 parte eſſet legittime impedita ãno ſeqñti vl̃ alias quiſp̃ïu potuerit mō ſili huiuſmodi Jeiuniuꝗ ſupplere teneaṝ Et ſi in toto vl̃ in parte adimplere cõmode nequeit eo caſu confeſſor ipm Jeiu-niium in alia pietatis opera ꝫmutet. Juxta q̃ in bulla dicti d̃ñi papꝝ pij pleni9 cōnſetiṙ Jn cui9 teſtimoſum Sigillum p Reuendos prēsdños Reynbardõu Epm et Rudolphuꝝ decanu wōmacien pro hac Jndulgẽcia ordiatii ,put ſup l̃ eis a dicto dño pio ſumopōtifice é data facultas pñtib9 é appenſum Datum Añcdalpſſydie Sema Oenſis Apl̃if Anno d̃ñi.ꝩ.ccc.ſexageſſoſecũdo .

43 *Indulgence for Benefactresses of St Ciriacus in Neuhausen* (Mainz: Johann Gutenberg, before 10 April 1462).

woman named Anna Vogtin of Ellwangen on 10 April 1462. It still retains its pendant wax seal depicting St Peter, the patron of Worms Cathedral, flanked by St Cyriacus with his palm frond on the left and the armoured St Viktor with his banner on the right, with the escutcheon of Count Reinhardt I von Sickingen, Bishop of Worms, below. Why was St Viktor invoked here? Because the co-sponsor of the indulgence, along with the Bishop of Worms, was Rudolf von Rüdesheim, Dean of both Worms Cathedral and St Viktor near Mainz, where Gutenberg was en-rolled as a lay-brother. It is possible that the indulgence was printed for Rudolf von Rüdesheim, co-patron of the Giant Bible of Mainz, within the grounds of St Viktor itself.

It appears that Gutenberg was one of the four printers who were conducting profitable work at the beginning of the 1460s. Here modern legends of his destitute state after the completion of the 42-line Bible fall apart, as they depend upon two historical fallacies: the supposed willingness of the Mainz law courts to enforce Fust's inopportune confiscation of all the assets earned for their 'common benefit', and a stubborn refusal to identify Gutenberg as the printer of the Mainz *Catholicon*. But Gutenberg must have made *some* money from the sale of his share of 158 or more Latin Bibles, from the transfer of the DK typecasting tools to Bamberg and from the sale of scores of copies of the first printed Latin dictionary and at least two quartos valued by Church officials, ventures that were successful enough to require later reprintings. Although he and an investor named Martin Brechter had failed since 1458 to make modest interest payments to the Chapter of St Thomas in Strasbourg on a sixteen-year-old loan of eighty florins, this fact is perhaps more an indication of Gutenberg's carelessness than it is a proof of any financial distress. The inventor, now entering his early sixties, must have looked forward to some quiet years in which he might enjoy what the world had left to offer, and to reflect upon all that he, in turn, 'with the help of the Most High', had given to the world.

SIX

A Trojan Horse

eneas Silvius Piccolomini, who had marvelled at quires of printed Bibles at Frankfurt in 1454, accepted the triple tiara as Pius II in Rome four years later. Already by 1461 the pope was much displeased with the goings-on in Mainz. Archbishop Diether von Isenburg, elected in 1459, had won the support of the Mainz citizenry when he promised that the Church would pay its taxes to the heavily indebted city instead of tithes and tributes to the papacy. Diether long had favoured reform throughout the Church, which he believed could be fortified by means of general Church councils wherein common goals and concerns could be discussed. Busy with urgent German affairs, he had neglected either to appear before the new pope in Rome or to attend the Congress at Mantua, where Pius launched his campaign for renewed commitment to his stalled crusade against the Turks. In retribution for these slights and other tardiness, the pope made Diether's confirmation as archbishop contingent upon two pledges: to pay an annual tithe (one-tenth of the archiepiscopal income) to support the international war effort in the east, and to forfeit his unique prerogative to convene a general council of the German bishops. Undeterred, Diether petitioned to reduce his investiture fee by half (back down to the traditional 10,000 florins), defaulted on the costly Vatican bank loan that had been imposed to cover the fee, and assembled the Electors of the Palatine,

Trier and Brandenberg, and other sympathetic German princes and bishops, who resolved to convene a general council at Frankfurt that would end papal abuses once and for all. This final act of defiance earned Diether his excommunication. The pope demanded that he be replaced by Count Adolph II von Nassau, a canon of Mainz cathedral who came from a noble family that had grown accustomed to seeing its scions become archbishop; he had finished second to Diether in his bid for election to this higher dignity. Ever defiant, Diether remained in Mainz, precipitating a broad-ranging regional conflict.

To wage the Archbishops' War, each side conscripted not only armies but printing presses. Fust and Schoeffer published the first broadside of the engagement, the emperor's announcement from Graz on 8 August 1461 in which he approved of the pope's impending removal of Diether and the installation of Adolph II upon the archbishop's chair. In Tivoli on 21 August 1461 the pope issued his official bull deposing and excommunicating Diether and dispatched a letter to Adolph affirming his election to the archiepiscopacy; he also wrote a letter confirming these acts to the fearful clergy and civil officials of Mainz. Fust and Schoeffer printed the Papal Bull and the letters as broadsides for wider circulation soon thereafter. But these were far from the last words in this controversy. On 30 March 1462, in Diether's name, Conrad Humery appealed in print to the Imperial Estate to submit the matter to arbitration by a neutral princely tribunal. This was followed by Diether's desperate *Manifesto* contesting Adolph's legitimacy, a letter from Adolph that answered Diether's accusations, and, finally, a much earlier letter from Diether that the pope had ignored; Fust and Schoeffer again printed all four of the broadsides, not so much as propaganda as news reports. According to the *Mainzer Chronik II*, compiled between 1582 and 1612, the towering broadside of Diether's *Manifesto*, replete with citations of precendents from canon law, was published by 'the first printer of books in Mainz, Johann Gutenberg'.[1] However, the only examples that survive are from the press of Fust and Schoeffer. Gutenberg might have participated in this war of words, but we no longer have physical evidence that he did.

While these printed salvos prolonged the stalemate, setting local factions against each other, covert negotiations pursued by papal agents throughout Germany further undermined Diether's precarious position. In June 1462 the armies of the pro-Adolph coalition marched towards Heidelberg, but they were intercepted at Seckenheim on the last day of the month. The capture of Karl of Baden-Baden, Ulrich of Württemberg and Bishop Georg of Metz by Diether's allies provided large ransoms, but the battle itself was not decisive. However, four months later, just before dawn on Thursday, 28 October 1462, a band of Adolph's troops quietly scaled the imposing fortifications of Mainz itself. Coordinating with operatives inside, they threw open the inner and outer doors of the southern gate (the Gautor), allowing papal coalition forces and four hundred Swiss conscripts to pour into the city. The local 'traitors' probably expected that Adolph would ride into the city unopposed, but as the bell towers sounded the alarm, furious resistance arose. After several hours of street fighting more than 350 citizens – including Burgermeister Jakob Fust, the printer's brother – had lost their lives. Whole neighbourhoods had burned; one of the losses, the Fustenhaus, was possibly Johann Fust's residence. Just before the city was secured, Diether escaped across the Rhine with most of his entourage, but Conrad Humery, his secretary, was captured and imprisoned. Then began the indiscriminate plundering – the soldiers' payday. The following afternoon, the victorious archbishop at last rode into Mainz, tore up the city's ancient privileges, dissolved the council, removed the guilds from all affairs of government, swept away the special rights of the patriciate and ordered the surviving adult male citizens to gather in the main market square the following day, Saturday. Some eight hundred complied, believing that normalcy would return once everyone had sworn allegiance to the new archbishop. Once there, however, they found themselves surrounded by armed mercenaries, 'like sheep in a pen'. Adolph entered the square and rebuked the multitude for their disobedience to the pope and emperor, declaring their lives forfeit – a terrifying moment for all – before granting clemency in the form of banishment from the city, effective immediately and to last at least through the beginning of Lent the following February.

Was Gutenberg caught up among that throng of eight hundred who were driven out through the Gautor, leaving behind their wives, children, homes and possessions? Most historians have assumed so, not on the basis of specific documentation, but by reason that this was a general exile, and the fact that the Hof zum Gutenberg, the inventor's ancestral home, was turned over 'for life' to one of Adolph's allies, Conrad Wilvung, clerk of the municipal court. But Wilvung's good fortune was not a form of punishment for Gutenberg, as the printer had not owned the ancient mansion for which he was named since at least 1444, if indeed he had ever owned it. Moreover, Gutenberg likewise may have earned Adolph's favour: in 1465 the archbishop would reward the ageing printer with a pension in consideration of his 'faithful' service. In any case, the long prelude to civil war must have suggested to Gutenberg the advisability of decamping to the family estate in Eltville well before the fateful final days of October. Either as an exile or as a refugee, he succeeded in protecting his various typographical materials, tools and supplies, whatever they may have been, throughout the ordeal; upon his death in 1468 they reverted to Dr Humery, who, long since pardoned, promised the archbishop that they would remain in Mainz.

By Shrove Tuesday, 22 February 1463, the archbishop's heart had softened, and the exiles were allowed to reassemble outside the gates of Mainz. While fifteen were jailed for seditious acts and some four hundred known enemies were expelled again under the oath never to enter the city, about three hundred who had not taken up arms during the unrest were allowed to return to their families or to occupy vacant homes within the city. Gutenberg was free to return, and eventually he did so. Johann Fust likewise survived the chaos without irrevocable consequences. It seems that he and Peter Schoeffer, a non-citizen who may have been free to remain in Mainz, had been wise to pursue a neutral political course, printing broadsides on behalf of both of the contending archbishops. The prudent partners were thrice fortunate: first, to have concluded the printing of their two-volume Latin Bible eleven weeks before the Sack of Mainz; second, to have survived the October looting with their printing shop intact; and third, to have safely preserved the unsold copies of their Bible. The latter pair of miracles may be indications that Fust and Schoeffer too had remained in Adolph's good graces. Even so, the Bible of 14 August 1462 was to be the last product of their press until late 1463, when they published Latin and German pamphlets of the *Bulla cruciata contra Turcos*, which Pope Pius II had issued from Rome on 22 October 1463. No major books would come forth from a Mainz press until 1465, when Fust and Schoeffer issued the *Liber sextus decretalium* of Boniface VIII, that is, more essential canon law with surrounding commentary, and Cicero's *De officiis*, on civic duties, presented in a specially sized small folio format with imitation Greek letters fudging the requisite quotations in that language. Then, in 1466, during a momentous bookselling trip to Paris, where many of the Bibles of 1462 and the new Ciceros found homes, Fust took ill and died, apparently a victim of the plague that raged there during the autumn months. Thenceforth Schoeffer, who married

Fust's daughter Christina, was in charge of Europe's leading printing workshop.

Towards the end of this tumultuous period, one last piece of printing would emerge, like a phoenix rising out of the ashes, from the seemingly defunct *Catholicon* workshop. This was a small single-sheet indulgence issued in late 1464 on behalf of the Order of Trinitarian friars (illus. 44). Based on a bull issued by Pius II in 1459, the indulgence was intended to raise funds to secure the release of Christian captives held in Muslim lands. The text begins with the initial V that had been introduced in Gutenberg's 31-line Cyprus indulgence a decade earlier, and it gives emphasis to five single-word headings by means of a heavier, crowded typeface that is found nowhere else. The only surviving copy of this indulgence was notarized on 11 December 1464 for Symon de Lüttich, priest of the church of saints Vitus and Anthony at Bad Hersfeld in Hesse, north of Fulda.

Historians have always listed the commissary of the Trinitarian indulgence simply as 'Frater Radulphus', without further identification, but he was too important to be so easily dismissed: he was Radulphus de Vivario, or Raoul du Vivier (d. 1472), prior of the Couvent des Mathurins in Paris, who was elected Minister General of the Order of Trinitarian friars in 1460. Here Raoul du Vivier emerges as the first Frenchman who is known to have employed a printer. Indeed, he probably played a central role in the introduction of the first printing presses in France six years later. The Couvent des Mathurins regularly hosted the meetings of the theology faculty of the University of Paris, and by 1469 Raoul du Vivier must have known Johann Heynlin, prior of the Sorbonne, and Guillaume Fichet, librarian of the college, who in 1470 would establish printing at the Sorbonne. Two years later Raoul was succeeded as Minister General by his protégé Robert Gaguin, the recipient of Fichet's famous letter of 1471, which identified Gutenberg as the first to devise the art of printing.

44 Radulphus de Vivario, *Indulgence on Behalf of the Order of Trinitarian Friars* (Mainz: Johann Gutenberg, before 11 December 1464).

The Trinitarian Indulgence of 1464 may have been the last thing that Gutenberg ever printed. No further items from the *Catholicon* press in Mainz during his lifetime are known, and the books that would be published with the same types by the Bechtermünze press at Eltville beginning in 1467 made no mention of Gutenberg in their colophons. The next news that is heard of Gutenberg constitutes a final upturn in his fortunes: on 17 January 1465, in an unusual and perhaps surprising gesture, Adolph II of Nassau formally recognized Gutenberg's prior services and made him a pensioned courtier (*Hoffgesindt*) of the archbishopric:

> We, Adolph, elected and confirmed Archbishop of Mainz, acknowledge that we have considered the agreeable and voluntary service which our dear and faithful Johann Gutenberg has rendered to us and our bishopric, and have appointed and accepted him as our servant and courtier. Nor shall we remove him from our service as long as he lives; and in order that he may enjoy it the more, we will clothe him every year, when we clothe our ordinary suite,

ſeul und zu praeḣ· do erſchrack das volck gar ſere·
Darnaeḣ fur der veint fur den tempel und fur ſeinē
werck das es alles volck ſahe·Do ſprachē ſie zu da=
niel·Du boſer man · wie haſtu uns unſeren apt̄got
zu proeḣē·Darumb muſtu ſterbē· Und ſprachē zu
dem kunig·Setz in in das hol zu den leuē die freſẕ
in zu hāt·Aber wie wollē dieḣ nȳmer zu kunig ha=
ben·Do was dem kunig gar leit·darumb das er in
geſiehert het und erbeit dar widre piẕ zu naeḣt·Do
wolte ſie ſein nieḣt geraten und ẕwungē den kunig
und viln an in·Do ſprach er zu daniel dẏ got wire
dieḣ erloẕē·   Naeḣ dem ſazte ſie in unter die leuen·
die warn ym unterthā als got wolt wañ er was eȳ
heiliger man·Alſo lag er drei tag unter den leuen·
Do ſandt ym got ein engel zu troſt·Der engel vȧȵt
abacuck auff dem velde der trug ein hafen mit fleiſeḣ
und keẕ und prot das wolt er ſein ſehniteren prȳgē

45 Page from *Vier Historien von Joseph, Daniel, Judith und Esther*
(Bamberg: Albrecht Pfister, May 1462).

always like our noble men, and give him our court dress; also, we grant him twenty bushels of grain and two large barrels of wine for the use of his house, free of duty upon its arrival in Mainz, every year as long as he lives, on condition that he will not sell it or give it away, as has been promised in good faith by Johann Gutenberg himself. Eltville, on Thursday, St Anthony's Day, 1465.[2]

Honoured formally for his beneficial work on behalf of the archdiocese, the 'dear and faithful' servant cannot have been a refugee from the archbishop's political doghouse; nor is it likely that Adolph's gesture reflects a belated act of forgiveness. Given such a generous pension, in the form of essential household goods to be delivered duty-free to Mainz, Gutenberg cannot be envisioned (as in the past) as a forgotten, penniless victim of a partner's betrayal; if he still had old debts, now at last they would recede to manageable levels. Moreover, the conditions of his appointment mentioned no official duties or expectations of ongoing work. At this stage in his life, perhaps his late sixties, Gutenberg may have felt little compulsion to keep pursuing risky business ventures. It seems that he no longer considered the work of the books – compiling capital, assessing the market and managing a competitive printing shop – to be worth the uncertainty and daily stress. Finally secure in life's essentials, he appears to have been content to live out the remainder of his days in retirement.

Writing in 1471 of the arrival of printing in Paris, Guillaume Fichet had alluded to the 'new order of book-makers from Germany, who have poured forth everywhere (as from a Trojan Horse)'. Like Fichet, many must have taken note of the speed with which the typographic art was spreading. Mentelin was the first outside of Mainz, completing his Latin Bible in Strasbourg by 1460. By February 1461 a sharpened state of the DK types, recently used to print the 36-line Bible for the bishop in Bamberg, had become the property of Albrecht Pfister, the local bishop's former secretary. It was probably Pfister who had organized the work of the Bible, employing experienced printers from Mainz, but now he changed direction, using the Mainz typeface in combination with numerous woodcuts in the Nuremberg style to become Europe's first specialist in typographic picture books. Mainly vernacular German texts, Pfister's books were intended as much for lay diversion as for moral instruction: Ulrich Boner's book of fables, *Der Edelstein* (14 February 1461); the retellings of the *Biblia historiale* known as the *Vier Historien von Joseph, Daniel, Judith und Esther*, printed 'not long after' 1 May 1462 (illus. 45); Latin and German editions of the *Biblia pauperum* (*c.* 1462–3); Johannes von Tepl's *Ackermann von Böhmen* (not after August 1463), in which God adjudicates the legal complaint of an everyday Bohemian 'ploughman' (actually a scribe who ploughs rows with his quill) against Death, who has taken away his wife; and a German version of Jacobus de Theramo's *Consolatio peccatorum, seu Processus Belial* (*c.* 1463–4), Pfister's only book without pictures. Here the pagan lord Belial, serving as the Devil's advocate, presses the charge that Jesus Christ had trespassed upon Lucifer's rightful domain during the Descent into Hell.

Printing soon spread to other points on the map, at first anonymously and mysteriously. Towards the end of 1461, in time for New Year's Day 1462, someone in Vienna or its vicinity printed a vernacular broadside blood-letting calendar that was illustrated with simple woodcuts of the new moon and full moon, leaving blank spaces for the hours and minutes of the Moon's phases to be entered 'according to the true course over Vienna' on the appropriate day of the month (illus. 46). The entries written on the only surviving copy (at the Scheide Library) were calculated so accurately that they have been assigned to the illustrious astronomer Johannes Regiomontanus, who had departed from Vienna a few weeks earlier to reside in Italy. The squarish *textus quadratus* typeface of the Vienna Calendar is a clunky step-child of the DK types, except that the letters are significantly smaller, about the size of the 42-line Bible types. The same Gothic typeface also shows up in an anonymously

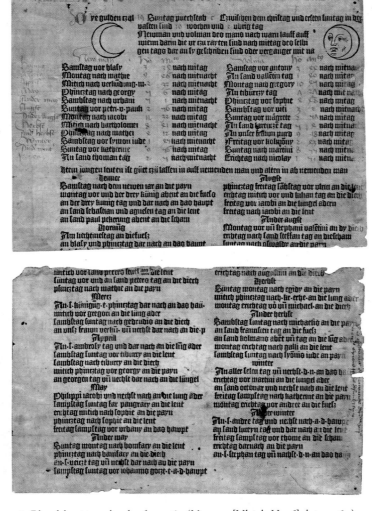

46 Blood-letting calendar for 1462 (Vienna: [Ulrich Han?], late 1461).

47 *Passione di Cristo* (North Italy: [Ulrich Han?], c. 1462–3).

printed German devotional booklet known as the *Seven Sorrows of the Virgin Mary* and a similar small-format *Leiden Christi* (or 'Passion of Christ'), both of which were illustrated with a selection of South German metalcuts that formerly had accompanied devotional manuscripts of the late 1450s.

The only printer of the 1460s who is known to have resided in Vienna is Ulrich Han, who set up a workshop in Rome before the end of 1466. Han's southward trek from Austria into Italy may be reflected by yet another unique and entirely mysterious piece of printing, the fragmentary *Passione di Cristo* (also at the Scheide Library), perhaps datable as early as 1462–3 (illus. 47). This small-format Italian-language version of the *Leiden Christi* – the first of all Italian printed books – was illustrated with the same German metalcuts but introduced a strangely bulky and primitive Gothic rotunda typeface (nearly as tall as the DK types) that loosely reflects a North Italian script. Each of these humble and somewhat homely little books shows a rudimentary understanding of the Gutenbergian printing system without a hint of Fust and Schoeffer's typographic refinements.

The Netherlands witnessed another anonymous and quite mysterious springing forth of printing in the aftermath of the unrest in Mainz, almost certainly at Utrecht. The earliest datable specimen of Dutch printing is a fragment of Alexander de Villa Dei's *Doctrinale* (c. 1465), which, like the Donatus, was a ubiquitous Latin school text (illus. 48). Its small, spiky *textus quadratus* typeface is now known as the 'Speculum' types, after the earliest intact Dutch printed book, the *Speculum humanae salvationis* (Mirror of Human Salvation, c. 1467), which was illustrated – in separate inking and printing operations – with woodcuts of typologically related episodes of the Old and New Testaments. Two other early Dutch typefaces are known as the 'Pontanus' and 'Saliceto' fonts. The former was used circa 1468, likewise probably in Utrecht, to print the *Singularia iuris* compiled by the Roman jurist Ludovicus Pontanus (1409–1439); it was issued with varying assortments of related legal tracts, including 'De

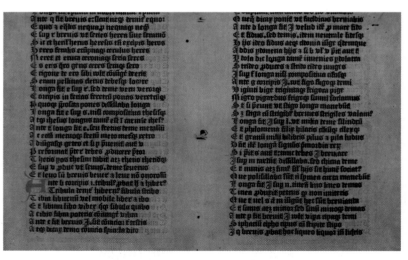

48 Alexander de Villa Dei, *Doctrinale* (Netherlands: Prototypography, c. 1465).

pravis mulieribus' by Pope Pius II. The 'Saliceto' font was used circa 1469 to print Guilelmus de Saliceto's *De salute corporis* (On the Sustenance of the Body) and various short tracts of Italian humanist origin, including the cautionary *De remedio amoris* (On the Cure for Love), which Aeneas Sylvius Piccolomini had written before he became Pius II. In each of the Pontanus and the Saliceto editions, the Dutch printers offered distinct 'packages' containing variable contents – a publishing strategy that enabled fifteenth-century purchasers to choose various combinations of reading material.

Perhaps the most important figures in the early diaspora of printers from Mainz were Conradus Sweynheym, a cleric in the archdiocese of Mainz, and Arnold Pannartz, a cleric in the diocese of Cologne – coincidentally, perhaps, the two centres of the Cyprus indulgence campaigns. It is easy to imagine that they had worked with Fust and Schoeffer until 1462, learning the essential tasks of printing while witnessing the enthusiastic reception that the *Durandus* of 1459 and the Clementine *Constitutiones* of 1460 received south of the Alps. Ultimately, the call that drew them to Italy arose from neither Rome nor any other flourishing city or noble court; rather, it came from the remote and venerable Benedictine Abbey of Santa Scolastica at Subiaco, a two-day journey east of Rome by way of Tivoli. At Subiaco during the summer of 1465, Sweynheym and Pannartz initiated a long series of Classical or theological editions, published in large quantities with the administrative and editorial support of Giovanni Andrea Bussi, Bishop of Aleria, a member of the papal curia. They began by printing an edition of Donatus, now entirely lost, soon followed by 275 copies each of Cicero's *De oratore* and Lactantius' *Opera*. Both used a small rounded Gothic typeface, while the Lactantius introduced the first legitimate Greek types (illus. 49). Two years later, in 1467, Sweynheym and Pannartz completed 275 copies of one of the truly essential works of

Christian thought, St Augustine's *De civitate Dei*. Later that year, recognizing the commercial advantages of an urban setting, the printers transferred their press to the Palazzo Massimi in Rome, where they printed editions of Cicero, Apuleius, Julius Caesar, Livy, Strabo and Pliny, as well as the letters of St Jerome and the first edition dedicated to poetry, the works of Virgil.

When Sweynheym and Pannartz arrived, the Eternal City already was home to the press of Ulrich Han of Vienna, who on 31 December 1466 had signed his name to Cardinal Johannes de Turrecremata's *Meditationes* on the life of Christ, the first major literary work by a living European author to appear in print. This handsome book featured 33 German-made woodcut illustrations based on the now-lost frescoes in the cloister of Santa Maria sopra Minerva, near the Pantheon, which had inspired Turrecremata's devotional text. Han then pivoted to the humanist market, using a smaller Roman typeface to print editions of numerous Classical authors, including Cicero, Ovid, Terence, Juvenal, Plutarch and Livy.

The metropolis of Cologne, well to the north of Mainz along the Rhine, had welcomed its first printer by 1466, when Ulrich Zel of Hanau in Hesse signed and dated his ten-leaf quarto edition of the first part of St John Chrysostom's *Super psalmum quinquagesimo, Miserere mei Deus* (that is, a sermon on Psalm 50, the fourth of the penitential psalms). Zel had matriculated at the University of Cologne in 1464, presumably to earn certain privileges that were necessary to conduct business as a printer. His press specialized in slender quarto-format tracts by such authorities as St Augustine, Cicero and the Sorbonne chancellor Jean Gerson, which could be bound together in various combinations for scholars, priests, or monastic or university readers. Although Zel's typographic lineage is made clear by the close resemblance of his first typeface to that of Fust and Schoeffer's Bible of 1462, his first-hand recollections of the invention of

Eclaraui ut opinor animam non esse solubilem. superest citare testes
quoꝗ autoritate argumēta firmēt̄. Neꝗ nūc, pphetas in testimoim
uocabo. quoꝗ ratio et diuinatio in hoc solo posita est: ut ad cultum dei et ad
imortalitatē ab eo accipiendā creari hominē doceant. sed eos pocius ꝗbus
istos qui respuūt ueritatē credere sit necesse. Hermes naturam describes ut
doceret ꝗadmodum esset a deo factus hęc intulit. καὶ αυτο εξ εκατε·
ρωρ φυσεωρ τησ τε αθαματορ και τησ θηρτησ μιαμ επο
ιει φυσιρ αμθρωπουτορ αυτορ πτη μερ αθαματορ πτη διε
θηρτορ ποιησασ και τουτορ φερωρ ερ μεσω θειασ και
αθαματορ φυσεωσ και τησ θηρτησ και ευμεταβλητου
ιδρυσερ ιρα ορωρ απαρτα απαρτα καιθαυμασͳ. Id est. Et
idem ex utraꝗ natura mortali et immortali unam faciebat naturam hōis:
eundem in aliquo ꝗdem imortalem in aliquo autē mortalē faciens: et hunc
ferens in medio diuinę et immortalis naturę. et mortalis mutabiliꝗ; coa-
stituit. ut omnia uidens omnia miret̄. Sed hunc fortasse aliquis in numero
philosophoꝗ computer. ꝗuis in deos relatus Mercurii nomine ab egiptiis
honoret̄. nec plus ei autoritatis tribuat: ꝗ Platoni aut Pictagore. Maius
igit̄ testimoniū regramus. Polites ꝗdam consuluit Appollinem Milesium:
utrū ne maneat anima post mortem an resoluat̄. Respondit his uersibus
ϯυχη μερ μεχρισ ου δεσμοισ προσ σωμα κρατειται φ-
θαρτα μοουσα παθη θηρτaισ αλγιδοσιρ εικει ηρικα δα-
μαλυσιρ ϸροτερμ μετα σωμα καραρθερ ωκισͳηρ ευρη-
ται εσ αιθερα πασα φορειται αιερ αρηφαοσ ουσ μερει διει-
σπαμπαματηρσ πρεστογορ ορος γαρ του το θεορ διεταξε
προπορια. Id ē passiōes sentiēs mortalibus cedit doloribus. Cū uero solu-
tōem būanā post corpus īuenies: facile abiens aeterra nūꝗ senescit. Aia ꝗdē
quo ad uinculis corporeis tenet̄ corruptibiles passiōes sentiēs. mortalibus
cedit doloribus. Cum uero humanā solutionem uelocissimā post corruptū
corpus īuenerit: omnis e terra ferē: nūꝗ senescens. et manet in eternis sine
pena. Primogenita eteni hoc diuina disposuit prudētia. Quid carmia sibil-
lina: Nōne ita eē declarant: cū fore aliquādo denūciant: ut a deo de minis
ac mortuis iudicet̄: quoꝗ exempla post inferemus. Falsa est igr̄ Democriti
et Epicuri sententia et dicearchi de animi dissolutione. ꝗ pfecto nō auderēt
de iterim aiarū mago aliquo presente disserere: ꝗ sciret certis carminibus
ciere ab inferis animas: & adesse et prebere se humanis oculis uidendas:
et loqui & futura pdicere. Et si auderent: re ipa et documentis presentibus

printing, as recorded in the Cologne *Cronica* of 1499, sidestepped Fust and Schoeffer to give unambiguous priority to Gutenberg and his Bible.

Strasbourg gained its second press in 1466, when Heinrich Eggestein, the former Keeper of the Seals for the bishopric, printed a Latin Bible in a rounded typeface that resembled Fust and Schoffer's 1462 Bible types. Eggestein may have become acquainted with Gutenberg during the latter's years in Strasbourg, and he appears to have visited Mainz himself between 1457 and 1459, returning to Strasbourg in time perhaps to assist with the foundation of Mentelin's press before establishing his own. After printing two additional Latin Bibles and a German version by 1470, Eggestein became Peter Schoeffer's direct competitor in the marketing of folio editions of canon law with commentaries.

In 1467 a printing workshop with direct lineage from Gutenberg's emerged in Eltville, a small town just across the Rhine to the northwest of Mainz, which was both the residence of Adolph II and the Gensfleisch family's ancestral home away from home. There the moveable preparatory types of the Mainz *Catholicon* of 1460, interspersed with odd sorts borrowed from the 31-line Cyprus indulgence font, last seen in 1455, were used to print an abbreviated Latin and German lexicon called the *Vocabularius ex quo*, which was derived from the *Catholicon*. The colophon of the *Vocabularius* states that it was begun by Heinrich Bechtermünze (one of Gutenberg's distant kinsmen), who died before the thick quarto was complete, and that it was completed by his brother Nicolaus Bechtermünze with the support of Wigandus Spyes on 4 November 1467. Nicolaus kept the Eltville press running intermittently for another thirteen years, reprinting the *Vocabularius* once in 1469 with the *Catholicon* types (illus. 50), and a second time in 1472 with a new typeface that closely resembles Gutenberg's old 31-line indulgence types. He used the latter types in a line-for-line reprint of the Mainz edition of the Aquinas

E p zelotipia e suspico uel furoz cu rone metis
accensus Eaa oz mulier que suspicone habz
zelotipiuz. vnere | oe viro
n, s zelotipus oz qsi zelo plenus et est idem cp
muidiosus uel suspicosus. Eaa oz vir q hz
suspicone sup mulierem suam leccatricem
m s zelus.i. muidia. amoz uel feruoz bonus siue
n s zemetu epn betoecke | malus
m s zephirus est nomen venti. west nozoen
zimos grece latine oz fermentu. vn azima
pm buq.papias. vero dicit zima fermentu
vn azima. Eaa ponif pzo peccato
zimzala pua musca scilicz culex
zizania qoam seges uel hezba puersa
n t zimciber qoam spes aromatica. pngwer
F p zona.i. cinguluz et ppe latu
m s zonarius est ille qui fadt zonas
n s zonifragium est zonaq fractio
m t zozobabel.i. iste magister oe babilone
m s zoncus.ca. cu.i. vitalis
m s zozimus.i. viuax uel viuidus. AOOEN

presens hoc opusculu no stili aut penne suf-
fragio sz noua artificiosacz inuentioe qua-
dam ad eusebiam dei monstrie per nicolau
bechtermutzeIn Eltuil est ofumatu Sub
anno domini OO.cccc lxix ipe die sci boni-
faci quj fuit quinta die mens Junij
Dinc tibi sancte nato cu flamine sacro
Laus et honoz ono trino tribuatur et vno
Qui laudare pia semp no linque mariam

50 *Vocabularius ex quo* in Latin and German (Eltville: Nicolaus Bechtermüntze, 5 June 1469), colophon.

Summa de articulis fidei (c. 1470) and in two further reprints of the *Vocabularius*, as well as at least four broadsides during the following decade.

Whereas the Eltville press used the *Catholicon* types in books dated 1467 and 1469, in February 1468 Dr Conrad Humery reassured Adolph II that the printing materials that Gutenberg left when he died would remain in Mainz and not be used elsewhere or sold. There is no contradiction here as long as Gutenberg or Humery had split up their assets before November 1467, some remaining in Mainz and some going to Eltville. While the Bechtermünze brothers took a modest supply of Gutenberg's individual types (but no slugs) to Eltville for the purpose of composing new titles, Humery retained 'numerous formes, letters, instruments, tools, and other items pertaining to the work of printing' in Mainz. These would have included the 49,000 metal slugs that had been prepared for reprinting the lucrative *Catholicon*, or perhaps some moveable types intended for the archbishop's use, or both. In the end, the *Vocabularius* was printed with moveable types in Eltville, while the *Catholicon* and the Aquinas and Matthaeus de Cracovia tracts were reprinted with slugs in Mainz.

By the beginning of 1468, a press was active in Augsburg. In March of that year Günther Zainer of Reutlingen completed a folio edition of the *Meditationes vitae Christi*, a perennially popular Franciscan devotional treatise, traditionally but incorrectly ascribed to St Bonaventure. As Zainer had gained citizenship in Strasbourg in 1463 by marrying the daughter of a burgher of that city, and long retained business connections with Strasbourg printers, it is nearly certain that he had learned to print in Mentelin's workshop. He remained a prolific printer, publishing some eighty editions – many richly illustrated with woodcuts – before his death in 1478.

Another press with a direct connection to Gutenberg started up in Nuremberg by 1470. Although some of the earliest editions from this press appeared without place, name or date, archival documents and colophons of others show that they were printed in Nuremberg by Johann Sensenschmidt and Heinrich Keffer. Their earliest publications included Franciscus de Retza's *Comestorium vitiorum* (dated 1470), a large folio on the Seven Deadly Sins, financed by the Nuremberg patrician

Heinrich Rummel; Albert Magnus, *Compendium theologicae veritatis* (c. 1470); Albrecht von Eyb's *Margarita poetica* (1472), the colophon of which identifies Johann Sensenschmidt as its printer; and the *Pantheologia* of Rainerius de Pisis (1473), which lists both Sensenschmidt and Keffer as its printers. Whereas the Helmasperger Instrument of 1455 had listed Keffer among the witnesses for Gutenberg, and an inscription in a copy of the early Catholicon-press *Dialogus* of Matthaeus de Cracovia records that Keffer was its donor, Sensenschmidt probably had assisted both Gutenberg in Mainz and Albrecht Pfister in Bamberg. Finally, the colophon in their edition of Retza's *Comestorium vitiorum* concludes with a direct quotation from that of the Mainz *Catholicon* of 1460: 'Nuremburge anno &c lxx°. patronarum formarum que concordia et proporcione impressus' – no doubt a veiled homage to Gutenberg.

A further pair of printers who appear to have been trained in Mainz were named together as witnesses in Mainz civil court documents of 1460 and 1461: 'Clas Götz und Hans von spyre die goltsmyd'. One Nicolaus Götz of Selestadt (Mentelin's home-town) had matriculated at the University of Erfurt in 1456 as an entering student and at the University of Cologne in 1470 in the law curriculum. Götz's datable editions range from 1474 to 1480, when he printed a modest Latin Bible that happens to have 42 lines per column. The other witness in Mainz, the goldsmith Johann von Speyer, would exert a much more lasting impact on the history of printing. Perhaps as early as 1462 he had left Mainz to joined the many German merchants in Venice, the great Adriatic seaport. There he married an Italian widow and fathered two children, including a daughter who had reached sufficient age to marry in 1477. By 1468 he must have been work-ing to establish a printing shop in Venice, and on 18 September 1469 he – 'Johannes de Spira' – learned that his application to the Signoria of Venice for a five-year monopoly on printing in the Veneto was successful. His petition had cited the 'universal acclaim' lavished upon two Classical editions that were already completed: Cicero's *Epistolae ad familiares* and a larger folio edition of Pliny's *Historia naturalis*, each signed and dated 1469. Within the same year he would reprint the Cicero in an edition of three hundred copies and undertake an ambitious folio edition of St Augustine's *De civitate Dei*, secure in the knowledge that he would have no local competitors for the right to print and export books by land or by sea. By way of comparison, Rome already was home to four different presses, operated by Sweynheym and Pannartz, Ulrich Han, Sixtus Riessinger and the first Jewish printers: Obadiah, Manasseh and Benjamin of Rome. But Venice's sole printer died during the production of the Augustine, which had to be completed in 1470 under the auspices of his brother and heir, Wendelin de Spira. By then others were clamouring for the right to print in Venice, and the Signoria wisely abolished the monopoly on printing. This was by no means unfair to Wendelin, who had inherited a flourishing printing enterprise, and it enabled the establishment of many new presses within the thriving port city.

Foremost among the early Venetian printers was the incomparable Nicolas Jenson, the former master of the royal mint in Tours, whom Charles VII of France was alleged to have dispatched to Mainz in order to learn the new typographic art. By 1470 Jenson had established the second press in Venice, which introduced a stately and beautifully balanced Roman typeface that appealed to Italian humanists as a worthy reflection of the *lettere antica* script and is justly admired to this day. Jenson's first book was a Latin translation of *De evangelica praeparatione* (Preparation for the Gospels) (illus. 51), originally written in Greek by Eusebius Pamphili, the fourth-century Bishop of Caesarea and 'Father of Church History', who argued for the superiority of Christianity over Roman paganism. Talented, prolific and adaptable, Jenson dealt well with his German competitors in Venice, forming the firm of Nicolas Jenson *et socii*, thereby remaining the leading printer in Venice during a decade in which the port city became the de facto capital of Europe's printing industry. He died there in 1480, a rich man.

Two further printers were trained in Mainz during Gutenberg's lifetime, although, like Jenson, they did not achieve independence as printers until later. One was Berthold Ruppel, whom the Helmasperger Instrument of 1455 had identified as Gutenberg's helper, 'Bechtolff von Hanau'. He introduced printing to Basel in the early 1470s. Another was Johann Neumeister, a cleric of Mainz, who, after perhaps visiting Rome, began printing at Foligno in Italy in 1470, where he published the first edition of Dante's *Commedia* in 1472. But Neumeister struggled to become anything more than the first 'wandering printer': fleeing from Foligno in serious debt, he was put under arrest in Rome in 1473; he moved thence (perhaps indirectly) to Mainz, where he printed a handsome illustrated edition of Turrecremata's *Meditationes* with a very Gutenbergian *textus quadratus* font in 1479; then suddenly to Albi in Languedoc in 1481; and finally to Lyon by 1483, where he slowly went out of business. There, listed as a

H oc Ienſon ueneta Nicolaus in urbe uolumen
  P rompſit:cui fœlix gallica terra parens .
S cire placet tempus?Mauro chriſtophorus vrbi
  D ux erat.æqua animo muſa retecta ſuo eſt .
Q uid magis artificem peteret Dux:chriſtus:et auctor?
  T res facit æternos ingenioſa manus .

.M.CCCC.LXX.

51 Eusebius of Caesarea, *De evangelica praeparatione* (Venice: Nicolaus Jenson, 1470), colophon.

pauper, the former printer evaded the dancing spectre of Death until 1512.

Knowledge of Gutenberg's invention probably came to Paris soon after 1455. Although no copy of the Gutenberg Bible is known to have reached Paris before the seventeenth century, copies of the Bible and the *Psalter* of 1457 were known elsewhere in France at early dates. The Vicar General of the Trinitarian friars in Paris commissioned an indulgence from Mainz in 1464, and six years later the Sorbonne established its first printing press under the aegis of two of its professors: Guillaume Fichet, who praised Gutenberg in his letter to Robert Gaguin, and, perhaps more important, Johannes Heynlin, recently arrived from the University of Basel, who invited three German-speaking printers, named Ulrich Gering, Martin Crantz and Michael Friburger, to settle in Paris, create a roman typeface and begin printing for the Sorbonne. Their first endeavour, the *Epistolae* of Gasparinus Barzizius (d. 1431) of Bergamo, which served the curriculum as a set of model Latin letters, appeared in 1470, self-proclaimed as the first book printed in France by the new 'German' method.

All the while, in Mainz, Peter Schoeffer continued his excellent work without Johann Fust. After his solo debut with the 'Second part of Part Two' of Aquinas's *Summa theologica* in 1467, he printed hundreds of editions over the next three decades, including the first edition of Emperor Justinian's *Institutiones* in 1468 (with the verse encomium to the three founders of typography), St Jerome's *Epistolae* in 1470, Gratian's *Decretum* in 1472, another Latin Bible in 1472, the *Decretales* of Pope Gregory IX in 1473, St Bernard of Clairvaux's *Sermones* in 1475, missals for Breslau in 1483 and Cracow in 1484, the illustrated herbal known as the *Gart de Gesundheit* in 1485, endless indulgences for the ongoing war against the Turks during the 1480s, another *Psalterium Benedictinum* with the old Psalter types in

1490, the illustrated *Chronecken der Sassen* in 1492, a missal for Mainz (which incorporated the old 42-line Bible types) in 1493 and another missal for Breslau that he signed in 1499. His sons and grandsons continued to print into the mid-sixteenth century.

Towards the end of Schoeffer's life, German scholars were still singing the praises of Johann Gutenberg and his invention. In 1499 Marsilius ab Inghen's compilation of humanist verse, *Oratio continens dictiones, clausulas et elegantias oratorias*, printed in Mainz by Peter von Friedberg, contained two Latin odes to the long-deceased printer. One by his kinsman Adam Gelthus was affixed to a public memorial:

> For the blessed inventor of the art of printing,
> (Sacred to the Most Great God)
> Johann Gensfleisch, discoverer of the art of printing,
> whose immortal name merits the highest praise from every
> nation and tongue, Adam Gelthus has placed his remains
> within the Church of St Francis at Mainz, where they rest
> in peace.[3]

Another was penned by the humanist Jacob Wimpheling, from Mentelin's home town, Selestadt:

> Blessed *Ansicare* [Gensfleisch], on account of you
> Germany is blessed and praised throughout the earth.
> Johann, in the city of Mainz, fortified by divine skill,
> you were the first to stamp with letters of bronze.
> Much do religion, the wisdom of the Greeks,
> and the Latin tongue owe unto you.[4]

Given that Schoeffer lived for another three years after these claims on Gutenberg's behalf appeared in print, he would have been able to contradict them if he saw fit. But he did not, just as he did not contradict the account of Gutenberg's invention in the Cologne *Cronica*, which was published in the same year; indeed, Schoeffer was content to allow three decades to pass after Gutenberg's death without challenging the story. Looking back, Schoeffer, Ulrich Zel, Gelthus, Wimpheling and others could see the broad reach of printing and speak of the praise owed by 'every nation' and heard from voices 'throughout the earth'. They were willing to see printing as something that was much larger than it was when Gutenberg last closed his eyes.

When the *Liber fraternitatis* of the Brotherhood of St Viktor recorded Gutenberg's passing, probably in February 1468, printing already had spread from Mainz to Strasbourg, Bamberg, Vienna (and somewhere in southern Germany and northern Italy), Utrecht, Subiaco, Rome, Cologne and Eltville. At that time early stages of typographic preparation would have been under way in Augsburg and Venice, where printed books would be published by 1469, and perhaps also in Paris, Nuremberg, Naples, Foligno, Trevi, Bologna, Basel and Beromünster in Switzerland. In 1471 printing exploded in breadth, adding more presses in the same towns and new presses in Speyer, Milan, Padua, Treviso, Ferrara, Florence, Mondovì, Verona, Perugia and perhaps others now forgotten. All of these printers would have either known Gutenberg or have worked with printers who had worked with him. But the next generations of printers, exemplified by William Caxton, who brought printing to Westminster in 1476, and the brilliant Venetian humanist-publisher Aldus Manutius beginning in 1495, probably learned their trade at third or fourth hand from subsequent printers who naturally would have modified what they had learned or introduced new methods. By the mid-1470s books were being produced with roman types, or in the Greek or Hebrew alphabets, with quire signatures, catchwords, folio numbers, musical notation, woodcut illustrations and maps; printers were impressing two page formes in a single pull of the press, advertising their wares by means of printed broadsides and transporting their books on the open sea; and by 1477 the Dominican nuns at San Jacopo di Ripoli in Florence were printing texts sacred and secular. None of these innovations had been attempted or perhaps even imagined by the late inventor in Mainz.

But Gutenberg had inspired all of these pioneer printers, at least indirectly, providing both the conceptual model and the first effective demonstration of cast moveable types for printing different texts repeatedly by means of a screw press. To return to Professor Fichet's apt Homeric metaphor, the newly invented 'wooden horse' – the printing apparatus – brought with it not destruction from within, but great light (*magnum lumen*) all around. This was accomplished not merely, or entirely, by a single pioneer (*Bonemontanus*), but by a whole new generation of booksellers (*novorum librariorum genus*) that followed him. Gutenberg lit the lamp that would illuminate humane learning throughout Europe, and yet it was the hard work of his growing number of disciples who passed the flame and kept it burning so brightly.

SEVEN

Gutenberg's Rescue

utenberg's reputation retained its high station at the dawn of the sixteenth century, but soon fortune's ever-turning wheel would relegate the printer to a deep and long-lasting obscurity.

In 1505 a distant relative, Ivo Wittig, a canon of St Viktor near Mainz and rector of the city's university (which today bears Gutenberg's name), reasserted his late kinsman's share of credit for the invention of printing, working him into the dedication to Emperor Maximilian of his German translation of Livy's *History of Rome*, 'printed in Mainz, the city in which the admirable art of printing was invented by the ingenious Johann Gutenberg in the year of Our Lord 1450, after which it was improved and perfected by the industry, expense and labour of Johann Fust and Peter Schoeffer in Mainz'.[1] This book was printed by none other than Fust's proud grandson, Johann Schoeffer, who was willing enough to put Wittig's words into print, but had both little reason to perpetuate Gutenberg's fame in other contexts and quite self-serving reasons to squeeze Gutenberg out of the story – which is exactly what he did ten years later in the chalice-shaped colophon that he composed for Tritheim's *Compendium sive Breviarium historiae francorum*:

In the year of our Lord 1515, on the vigil of St Margaret, in the noble and famous city of
Mainz, inventress of the typographic art, the printing of this chronicle was finished
by Johann Schoeffer, descendant of that honest man Johann Fust, a citizen of
Mainz, the first author of the aforesaid art. It was in the year 1450, during
the thirteenth indiction under the reign of the most illustrious Roman
Emperor Frederick III, with the reverend father in Christ, Prince-
Elector Theodoric, grand cup-bearer of Erbach, occupying the
archbishop's chair in Mainz, that this Johann Fust began to
devise and finally invent (solely by means of his own
genius) the art of printing. In the year 1452, aided
by divine favour, he had so far improved and
developed his craft that he was then able
to print; yet for many improvements
in this endeavour he was indebted
to the great ingenuity of
his assistant and
adopted son,

PETER

Schoeffer of
Gernsheim, to whom,
in acknowledgement of his many
services and his skill, he gave the hand of his
daughter Christina Fust. These two men, Johann Fust & Peter
Schoeffer, carefully kept this art secret for their own advantage; and thus
they demanded from their workmen and servants an oath that the method should never
be divulged. Despite this precaution, in the year 1462 the workmen carried knowledge of this
art to distant countries, and thereby initiated its wide development.[2]

Without direct heirs, venerable disciples or local champions to promote his memory, Gutenberg soon receded ever further from the glare of fame. While subsequent generations ignored crucial facts and entrenched multiple campaigns of misinformation, local patriots in various towns pushed alternative 'inventors' into the discussion. Claims on behalf of Fust and/or Schoeffer were repeated often enough in sixteenth-century Mainz that they were widely accepted as established fact. The internationally renowned scholar Erasmus of Rotterdam considered Fust and Schoeffer to be the inventors of printing. The main objection came from Strasbourg, where in 1521 the local humanist Hieronymus Gebwiler asserted in his *Panegiris Carolina* – no doubt at the instigation of the local printer Johann Schott – that the true inventor was Schott's maternal grandfather, Johann Mentelin. Gebwiler's claim was amplified by Mentelin's descendant Jacob Mentel in *De vera typographiae origine* (Paris, 1650). Although Mentelin got into print about as early as one could outside of Mainz, there is no evidence that he was a founding innovator of the early 1450s. Regardless, two centuries after the actual events, the conversation had moved away from Gutenberg, creating a vacuum in which facts had little purchase; the honour attached to the invention of printing was essentially up for grabs.

A stubbornly persistent claim on behalf of Dutch typographic priority originated in Haarlem during the 1560s. This campaign doubtless arose from the vague suggestion in the Cologne *Cronica* that typography in Mainz had a mysterious 'Dutch prefiguration' – some manner of alternative, unnamed bookmaking – probably having to do with blockbooks. In the first known telling of this story, Volckertsz Coornhert's preface to his Dutch translation of Cicero's *Officia ciceronis* (Haarlem, 1561), an unnamed citizen of Haarlem was the first to print books, but his invention was stolen by an apprentice who took it to Mainz.

A generation later, Adrian de Jonghe (Hadrianus Junius) embellished the tale in his patriotic book *Batavia* (Leiden, 1588), fabricating an impossibly early printing career for a local Haarlemer named Laurens Janszoon Coster. Supposedly printing books with metal types on presses by 1428, Coster was said to have lost everything on Christmas Eve in 1440 when his unfaithful servant, named Johannes Faustus, mustered both the muscle and the logistical wherewithal to steal his master's presses, matrices and metal types and to set up his own successful shop in Mainz. Clearly the fabricators of the 'Coster Legend' had no idea who Johann Fust of Mainz was, other than an impediment to their patriotic purposes. They found it useful to bring him to Haarlem only to recast him as a servant and a thief – and thereby exposed their own fraudulence.

Although Gutenberg's renown eventually was obscured by that of pretenders, he was not entirely forgotten. In 1541 Johannes Arnoldus Bergellanus, who served as the corrector of Franz Behem's press at St Viktor near Mainz, published a Latin ode to the local invention of printing, *De chalcographiae inventione poema encomiasticum*, in which he identified Gutenberg as the 'primus typographiae inventor'. Bergellanus presented Gutenberg's colleague, called Johann Faust, as the supplier of money for the printing of the first books, while another colleague, Peter Schoeffer, deserved credit for introducing an improved method of producing metal letters by means of a casting matrix. This treatment of Schoeffer's technical role accords extremely well with what is known about the early development of typecasting techniques in Mainz, which at first had not utilized permanent casting matrices. Moreover, Bergellanus appears to have had access to important documents in Mainz, as his definition of Fust's financial role demonstrates an awareness of the legal settlement of 1455.

André Thévet's *Les vrais pourtraits et vies des hommes illustres*, published in Paris in 1584, was notable not only for introducing what remains the most recognizable and influential of the many 'portraits' of Gutenberg, but for preserving the faded memory that he had invented typography, an event that Thévet dated to 1442. Although Thévet's brief entry did not pretend to know much of anything about the inventor or his work – nor was the compiler quite sure who the early printers 'Jean Fauste' or 'Yves Scheffey' were (Peter Schoeffer's grandson was named Ivo) – it praised the cultural value of printing, provided an overview of its subsequent geographic spread and considered the notion that unreported precursors of European printing had been seen by Marco Polo in China.

A somewhat forgotten source regarding the invention of printing was a Jesuit schoolbook by Jacobus Pontanus called *Progymnasmatum latinitatis* (Ingolstadt, 1592), dozens of editions of which were read by thousands of schoolboys across northern Europe. It identified Germany's two greatest inventors as Berthold Schwarz, an alchemist said to have developed gunpowder (!) in 1380, and Gutenberg:

> In the year 1440 since Christ's godly birth, during the reign of Frederick III, Johann Gutenberg, a man of knightly nobility, invented at Mainz the method of writing in bronze types. From small beginnings this craft of human genius soon reached the highest level of perfection. His divine discovery is indeed worthy of admiration, for it can scarcely be believed that in a single day one man can form as many letters as the fastest scribe can write in two years.[3]

Meanwhile, as the sixteenth and seventeenth centuries progressed, even those who knew about Gutenberg's claim to fame retained no memory or awareness of the Latin Bible that was described as the first of all printed books in the Cologne *Cronica* in 1499. Demand for updated vernacular translations of the scriptures during the Reformation and the availability of countless newly printed Latin Bibles for Catholic worship had made the first edition of circa 1455 entirely obsolete. The question of where a copy might be found would not have occurred to anyone. While close to fifty of them had turned into sleeping beauties on forgotten shelves, long neglect and active disregard had imperilled more than one hundred others that cannot be found today. Eventually at least fifteen of the Bibles came to subsist as meagre fragments, their vellum or paper leaves having been sliced into pieces by unthinking bookbinders for purposes of recycling them as wrappers, liners, guards and strips to enclose or reinforce newer books (illus. 52). For the impecunious bookbinder, using blank parchment or paper was wasteful and too costly; it was cheaper simply to cut up stacks of disbound leaves bearing Gutenberg's innovative artistry.

At least one of Gutenberg's Bibles had a brush with fame in this dark period. In 1588 the vellum copy that is today at the University of Göttingen was spotted in the ducal library of Julius of Braunschweig-Wolfenbüttel. Although Eberhard Eggelinck's inventory correctly identified it as the earliest edition from the very beginnings of printing, there was no mention of Gutenberg: 'The Latin Bible, first and second part, printed on vellum in the very first and oldest edition, when printing had just started. In folio, bound with boards in yellow soft leather and furnished with brass studs and clasps.'[4] In 1618 this same Bible, transferred from Wolfenbüttel to the University of Helmstedt, again was catalogued as the first edition. This time, however, it was ascribed to a particular printer: 'Latin vulgate Bible, the Old and New Testaments, printed by Johann Faust (Mainz, 1460). Two vols., the first edition, very splendid and very rare, printed on vellum, with initials colourfully decorated and illuminated.'[5] During the 150 years since the true inventor's death, Fust clearly had enjoyed

52 A vellum leaf of the Gutenberg Bible used as a binding for a German law book, *c.* 1666.

better press – good enough to convince well-informed university librarians to substitute his name for that of Gutenberg.

The haphazard and dubious early historiography of the invention of printing took a somewhat misdirected but ultimately positive turn in 1620. The owner of an original copy of the Helmasperger Instrument, Johann Friedrich Faust von Aschaffenburg, a patrician in Frankfurt am Main who mistakenly believed that he was related to Johann Fust of Mainz, produced a Latin retelling of the 'work of the books' in which he (probably intentionally) transposed the roles of the protagonists, so that Fust emerged as the inventor of typography while Gutenberg took on the lesser role of the investor who litigated the repayment of his loans. This garbled version was first published in Guido Panciroli's *Nova reperta sive Rerum memorabilium recens inventarum* (Frankfurt am Main, 1631), a general work on human inventions. Bernhard von Mallinckrodt, dean of Münster Cathedral, recognized the importance of this early episode, and in his lengthy history of the rise of printing, *De ortu et progressu artis typographicae* (Cologne, 1640), he drew scholarly attention to the corroborative authority of the two earliest witnesses to the origins of European printing: just as the Cologne *Cronica* credited Gutenberg as the inventor of printing around 1450, so the Mainz lawsuit demonstrated that Fust and Gutenberg were producing books together prior to 1455. Thus the Baroque frontispiece to Mallinckrodt's book (illus. 53) paired Gutenberg's

53 Bernhard von Mallinckrodt, *De ortu et progressu artis typographicae dissertatio historica* (Cologne: Johannes Kinchius, 1640), engraved title page.

imaginary likeness with Fust's, as each of them was, irrefutably, a co-founder of the earliest printing press in Mainz. At last typography was a worthy subject for a historian, and Gutenberg's career could become, for the first time, the subject of serious study, although there were counter-claims from Strasbourg, Haarlem and Mainz itself to deal with first.

Vindication of Gutenberg and his stolen glory began in 1741, with the publication of Johann David Köhler's *Hochverdiente und aus bewaehrten Urkunden wohlbeglaubte Ehren-Rettung Johann Guttenbergs* (The Highly Deserved and Document-Certified Rescue of Johann Gutenberg's Honour). A professor of history at the University of Göttingen, Köhler compiled a convincing array of fifteenth-century archival sources from Mainz and historical references to Gutenberg, Fust, Schoeffer and Mentelin in early chronicles which demonstrated that Gutenberg had both the earliest and the best claim to be the authentic inventor of European typography. Moreover, Köhler was the first to reveal the true nature of the Mainz litigation of 1455: whereas Fust had provided major loans for ink, paper, parchment and a costly apparatus several years prior to 1455, Gutenberg was responsible for developing the apparatus and running the 'work of the books'. Next to Köhler's work, the claims for other inventors suddenly looked ill-formed and derivative. But a key point had eluded Köhler: doubting the well-chronicled evidence from 1499 that Gutenberg's first book was a lost Latin Bible printed with large letters, Köhler figured that Fust and Schoeffer's Bible, signed and dated 1462, was the ultimate outcome of Gutenberg's doomed first venture. For Köhler, Gutenberg was indeed the inventor of printing, but the hunt for his first book was over.

Unbeknownst to Köhler, the ongoing search for Gutenberg's Bible had already begun to bear fruit elsewhere. Between 1696 and 1702 Christoph Hendreich (illus. 54), head of Berlin's Electoral Library, had inscribed that library's illuminated vellum

42-line Bible with the key passages concerning the Bible from the Cologne *Cronica* of 1499 and Johannes Tritheims' *Annales Hirsaugienses* (published in 1690). This indicates that Hendreich considered the undated Bible, printed with large Gothic letters like those in fifteenth-century missals, to be the first of all editions – that is, the one printed by Gutenberg. To Hendreich, therefore, goes the honour of being the first person (that we know of) who was able to look past Gutenberg's centuries of documentary oblivion and speak of a specific 42-line Bible as Gutenberg's Bible. Local discussions of the Bible culminated in 1747 with Melchior Ludwig Widekind's article in the journal *Berlinische Bibliothek*, in which the young Protestant minister described it in no uncertain terms as Europe's earliest typographic Bible.[6] This was met with mild interest by a few local historians but did little to elevate Gutenberg's fame more broadly.

Already in 1745, the Swiss librarian Samuel Engel became the first to publish a definitive identification and description of Gutenberg's long-missing Bible. On the last day of July in 1744, during a visit to the library of the Carthusians of Michaelsberg just outside of Mainz, Engel had discovered (with no help from the oblivious librarian) the 42-line Bible that in 1781 would become the property of the Archbishop of Mainz and now resides in nearby Aschaffenburg. Engel believed that this Bible, printed with 'Missal' types, was the earliest of all editions and had been donated by Gutenberg himself. He published his breakthrough recognition in the *Journal helvètique*, but somehow it was never cited and appears to have been entirely forgotten until 2017.[7] More impactful discoveries soon followed. In 1760 Abbot Martin Gerbert of the Benedictines of St Blaise in the Black Forest surmised that his monastery's vellum 42-line Bible (now in the Library of Congress in Washington, DC) must have been Gutenberg's work, and in 1761 Baron Gerard Meerman of Rotterdam agreed that the vellum 42-line Bible owned by the

54 Christoph
Hendreich
(1630–1702),
Royal Librarian
in Berlin,
engraving,
1733.

CHRISTOPHORVS HENDREICH
SER. EL. BRAND. A CONSILIIS
ET BIBLIOTH.

G.P.Busch sculps Berol, 1733.

Benedictines of Mainz (now in the Bibliothèque nationale in Paris) must be the earliest of all.[8] In 1763 the Parisian bookseller Guillaume-François de Bure declared that the paper copy of the 42-line Bible in the library of Cardinal Jules Mazarin in Paris was the earliest of all printed Bibles, although not as early as a considerably scruffier Dutch printing of the *Speculum humanae salvationis*. Setting the discussion back about sixty years, de Bure attributed Mazarin's Bible to Johann Fust, with no mention of Gutenberg. De Bure's catalogue of this great Parisian library reached an international audience, and so, for no tenable reason (why name something after a German when you don't have to?), the 42-line Bible came to be known throughout Europe by its new French byname: the *Bible Mazarine*.

Discussion of Europe's first printed book could not proceed fruitfully without resolving its most nagging problem: for more than a century librarians had been uncovering *two* different unsigned, undated fifteenth-century folio Bible editions, both of which were printed with large 'Missal' types. One edition featured very large *textus quadratus* types arrayed in columns of 36 lines of text. It was represented by Bibles discovered at Bamberg and several monastic sites well to the east of Mainz, one copy of which had been dated by its rubricator in 1461, the same year that Albrecht Pfister began using the same types to print German picture-books in Bamberg. Its large Gothic types (which we recognize as the DK types) were formidably early: in 1766 Meerman noticed that they also appeared as the headings in the 31-line Cyprus indulgences dated 1454 or 1455. It seemed unavoidable that the 36-line Bible should also be assigned to the cradle of printing in Mainz. Meanwhile, the other ancient edition, the *Bible Mazarine*, featured columns of 42 lines of slightly smaller *textus quadratus* types and was represented by copies found in the libraries of the Benedictines of Mainz, the Carthusians of Mainz, the Archbishop's Seminary in Mainz and in numerous libraries up and down the Rhine and further to the east. The Seminary copy, now in Paris, was rubricated in August 1456 by Heinrich Cremer, vicar of St Stephen's in Mainz. Recognizing that this meant the 42-line Bible was anterior to the earliest dated printed book (the Mainz *Psalter* of 1457), Jean-Baptiste Maugerard, a noted Benedictine librarian (and plunderer of monastic libraries) purchased the neglected Bible at a bargain price and published his discovery in Metz in 1789, declaring that Europe's earliest printed book was *la Bible . . . de Guttemberg.*[9]

By the Revolutionary year of 1789, Gutenberg was again something of an international hero. Ten of his Bibles had been identified, a dozen more would be found during the following decade, and antiquarian-minded librarians and a new breed of highly acquisitive book collectors were on the lookout for more. These wealthy bibliophiles, mainly French or British (but hardly ever German), were not at all interested in the scriptures, but rather in the origins of printing, particularly the early landmarks that presented the most challenging quarry. Foremost among the early private collectors was George John, 2nd Earl Spencer, who committed exorbitant time and treasure to a love of antiquarian books. His interests originally centred on the Classics, such as the 1469 *editio princeps* of Virgil, but in 1790 he paid the impressive sum of £340 to the London book-seller Thomas Payne Jr for a superbly illuminated 42-line Bible (from the Augustinians of Colmar in Alsace, now at the Rylands Library in Manchester), Fust and Schoeffer's *Psalterium Benedictinum* of 1459 and Mentelin's German Bible of 1466. By 1801 Spencer was collecting not only Pfister's vernacular picture books, but Cyprus indulgences – about as far from Virgil as one can get. Through the efforts of bibliographically astute agents searching monastic libraries abroad, as well as the writings of the enthusiastic biblio-publicist Thomas Frognall Dibdin, the earliest typographic monuments became essential trophies for all true connoisseurs.

Just as the printed relics of the long-dead hero of Mainz could entertain the leisurely interests of the British nobility, so too could his memory serve the causes of *liberté*, *égalité* and *fraternité*. Addressing the Revolutionary Convention in Paris on 9 September 1792, Anacharsis Cloots, the Prussian-born baron turned radical, called for Gutenberg's 'apotheosis' within the Panthéon in Paris to honour 'the memory of that first Revolutionary, the premier benefactor of humanity'.[10] Hearing of the 'liberation' of Mainz by the French forces under General Adam Philippe de Custine on 21 October 1792, Cloots encouraged the victor to transfer the urn with Gutenberg's ashes from Mainz (along with his 'famous Bible') to a worthy resting place in the Panthéon. Alas, this mission was doomed to fail, as Gutenberg's remains, so long ago interred in the cemetery of the Barefooted Franciscans, proved impossible to locate following the Prussian bombardment the following spring. Similarly, no copy of the 42-line Bible could be found in the city, the clever Maugerard having bought one copy for himself and the apprehensive archbishop having just evacuated another to Aschaffenburg. Undaunted, Pierre Lebrun-Tondu, the French foreign minister, directed his generals throughout the occupied Rhineland to requisition worthy library treasures, notably *la Bible de Gutenberg*, for transfer to Paris. None of those that were found actually made their way to the Bibliothèque nationale in Paris, which already had acquired two copies through the ubiquitous agency of Maugerard; these Bibles made their way instead to auctions and wealthy collectors.

Following close upon the impassioned rhetoric of Cloots, Georg Christian Gottlieb Wedekind, a Mainz physician and leader of the local Jacobin Club, proposed the creation of a suitable public monument to Gutenberg – not in Paris, but in Mainz.[11] Nothing materialized until 1827, when the Casino Society of Mainz, irked by Haarlem's celebration of the Laurens Coster quadricentennial in 1823, commissioned the local sculptor Joseph Franz Scholl to carve a statue of the inventor for the courtyard of the Casino, the former site of the Hof zum Gutenberg (illus. 55); it is now in the Gutenberg Museum in Mainz. Bearded and wearing flowing Renaissance garb, the rather stunted and soulless sandstone figure proffers a small rectangular plate that bears the Gothic letters 'ABC' while a scroll bearing the plans for a printing press unfurls by his side; hefty books lie at his feet. The Latin legend carved on the base reads (in translation): 'He who was the first of all to discover the printing of letters in metal, on account of this art, well deserves the immortal memory of his

JOANNI GENSFLEISCH

55 Joseph Franz Scholl, *Joanni Gensfleisch dicto Gutenberg*, 1827, stone.

name throughout the whole world.' It may be a competent statue, but few would take notice of it were it not of Gutenberg. More-over, its modest scale and private location did not satisfy the growing desire for a more public and artistically worthy monument to the miraculous man of Mainz.

To that end in 1833 a civic 'Commission formed for the erec-tion of the public monument to Johannes Gutenberg' signed a contract with Bertel Thorvaldsen, the famous Danish sculptor, for a larger-than-lifesize bronze statue to be delivered to the market square in Mainz (illus. 56).[12] The idealized Neoclassical figure assumes a powerful stance high upon his pedestal, his left hand clutching to his breast a thick folio in a Gothic binding – implausibly inscribed (in German) 'The Bible printed by Gutenberg' – and his right hand holding a fistful of type punches. While his heavy cloak hangs like Classical robes, his shirt and high-waisted trousers cling tightly to his physique, suggesting heroic vigour. Most remarkable is the determined and mighty Homeric head, enlarged with a fur-lined cap, flowing hair, a flared moustache and a long bifurcated beard, all of which canonized the fictive French portrait made for Thévet's 'illustrious men' in 1584. Bronze plaques adorn the three approachable faces of Thorvaldsen's stone pedestal: one depicts the invention of move-able types; the second shows the press in action; and the third is inscribed in Latin to the effect that in 1837 all of Europe had gathered to honour this great citizen of Mainz. Unfortunately, bibliophiles who had anticipated a chance to admire Gutenberg's epochal masterpieces in his hometown were disappointed, as the municipal library possessed but a single vellum binding scrap of the Bible that Thorvaldsen had portrayed in bronze.

More celebrations of Gutenberg followed in 1840, the sup-posed fourth centenary of Gutenberg's invention. Strasbourg erected its own monument in the Place Gutenberg, and on *Johannistag* (24 June), the Bookseller's Exchange in Leipzig,

Germany's leading centre for publishing and bookselling, staged a massive festival for which Felix Mendelssohn composed two works, his Symphony No. 2 in B flat, to be performed in the St Thomaskirche, and a festival anthem for the market square, featuring paired men's choirs, two hundred voices strong, with sixteen trumpets, twenty trombones and kettledrums. This *Festgesang* set music to a patriotic poem by Adolf Eduard Prölss that recast the inventor's achievement as a golden dawn that welcomed the German people out of darkness. Mendelssohn's stirring tune is more famous in its reincarnation as the English Christmas carol 'Hark! The Herald Angels Sing'.

Gutenberg scored another posthumous victory in 1890, when the tenuous claims for the priority of the 36-line Bible at last were put to rest. In that year Karl Dziatzko, librarian of the University of Göttingen, demonstrated that two major textual errors in the 36-line edition came about when its compositors became careless with their copytext, which was none other than the 42-line Bible. The first, a garbled reading of *et angelus domini vocatus est* at the end of 4 Ezra, chapter 1, showed that they had misunderstood the peculiar partial-line 'runover' of the same passage in the 42-line Bible (illus. 57); the second (later corrected in all but the Stuttgart copy) was the disastrous omission of all the text (Genesis 8:11 to 11:2) that should have been copied from f. 8 in the 42-line Bible, which was either missing from the model copy or was skipped by the page turner. Clearly, the 42-line edition already existed when the printing of the 36-line edition began. At last, there was only one true Gutenberg Bible.

Nevertheless, in the 1890s the traditional Mainz origins of European printing came into question once again with the discovery in Avignon of legal documents of 1444 to 1446 concerning Procopius Waldfogel, a metalsmith from Prague. On 4 July 1444 Waldfogel had contracted to provide local investors with two steel alphabets (*abecedaria*), two iron forms (*formae*), a steel object called a 'vine' (*vitis*, possibly a screw), 48 more tin forms and other items pertaining to writing (*artem scribendi*).[13] Further, on 10 March 1446 Waldfogel agreed to supply Davin de Caderousse with 27 iron Hebrew letters (presumably 22 basic letters and alternate terminal forms of kaf, mem, nun, pe and tsadi) and various other metal and wooden implements in exchange for Davin's secrets for dyeing cloths with pigments. In April 1446 two students sold back their implements of various metals and wood, testifying that Waldfogel's *arte artificialiter scribendi* was a true art that was worthwhile for anyone who applied himself to it or enjoyed using it. Many scholars have accepted Waldfogel's short-lived enterprise in Avignon as a precursor or true origin of European typography, particularly as they take *arte artificialiter scribendi* to mean the 'art of writing artificially'. But the Latin adverb *artificialiter* does not imply that something unnatural, surrogate, fake or deceptive was made (as in 'artificially flavoured'). In the fifteenth century the term meant artfully, skilfully, cunningly or scientifically. In the colophon of the Mainz *Psalter* (1457), *adinventione artificiosa imprimendi* meant the 'artful invention of printing', while in Jenson's 1471 Quintilian, the words *impressit artificio* praised his skilful printing; in Johann Zainer's 1474 Ulm edition of Petrus Berchorius, *artificialiter effigatus* implied not that Zainer had made the book artificially, but rather that he had made it well. Waldfogel's mysterious enterprise was designed to improve a scribe's work, not to replace it; there was no mention of pressing or stamping, or of books of any sort, much less of multiplying them. Nevertheless, the unkillable legend that Waldfogel invented a process for printing still echoes today in the baseless assertion that Gutenberg was merely one of many Europeans of the 1440s who were racing to invent 'artificial writing'. In contrast to those 'other pioneers' who failed to leave us a single scrap of printing, Gutenberg

56 Bertel Thorvaldsen, *Joannem Gensfleisch de Gutenberg*, 1836, bronze, Gutenbergplatz, Mainz.

57 Proof that the Gutenberg Bible served as the copytext for the 36-line Bible. In Karl Dziatzko, *Gutenbergs früheste Druckerpraxis* (1890), plate VIII (enhanced for clarity).

created indulgences, Donatus editions, pamphlets and folio Bibles that have survived by the dozens.

By the end of the nineteenth century – despite all the past controversies – Gutenberg had been given due credit for the invention of European typography and the printing of the 42-line Bible. His achievements had been celebrated around Europe, his books had been treasured and studied like no others, and the cultural impact of his invention had been memorialized in multiple statues and stirring anthems. In the year observed as the quincentenary of his birth, 1900, the proud citizens of Mainz founded both the Gutenberg Society and the Gutenberg Museum, where the newly discovered *Sibyllenbuch* fragment and two 42-line Bibles would reside. Keen-eyed German bibliographers studied Gutenberg's books and types in painstaking detail. Between 1847 and 1926, ten copies of the Bible arrived in the United States, three of them – a vellum copy, an illuminated Old Testament and a superbly preserved paper copy – acquired by John Pierpont Morgan. In 1930 the United States government, convinced of the cultural necessity of Gutenberg, voted to allocate funds to purchase – from a crypto-Nazi named Otto Vollbehr – a fine vellum specimen of the Bible for the Great Hall of the Library of Congress, where it has remained on display almost continuously ever since. In that same decade the *idea* of Gutenberg, long a legitimate source of pride for German people, was conscripted by the Nazi Party to serve as a figurehead for their racist theories of German superiority; exhibition catalogues doubled as propaganda, and a genius for invention was trumpeted as a particularly German trait. Once again, in 1940 (under the cloud of worldwide conflict), and in 1950, 1955 and 1968, traditional Gutenberg anniversaries were celebrated with festivals, exhibitions and commemorative publications. During this period, top specialists concluded that a rare *Missale speciale* acquired by the Morgan Library in 1953, printed with an incomplete set of the smaller Mainz *Psalter* types, was even earlier than the 42-line Bible. This Gutenbergian missal was announced as Europe's oldest printed book in the 1 March 1954 issue of *Life* magazine, but eventually innovative paper analysis proved that it was the work of a middling epigone of the 1470s, working in Basel.[14] Telling discoveries continued: in 1982 the forgotten method of printing the different issues of the '1460' *Catholicon* with slugs came to light, and as the new millennium dawned, Paul Needham and Blaise Agüera y Arcas, a graduate student at Princeton University, determined that Gutenberg's typecasting invention had not functioned as had been believed for centuries – each letter was not one of many identical children of a punch and its matrix, but was a unique casting of diverse elements based on the 'strokes' that a scribe would use to construct them.[15] Even though the definition of what Gutenberg had invented required new scrutiny, his status as its inventor remained unchanged.

By then Gutenberg had been named 'Man of the Millennium', his influence had been discussed in an endless number of media outlets, and his career had been celebrated again and again in publications and exhibitions in Mainz and around the world. Meanwhile, new fragments from his press have come to light in old bindings, and serious scholarship on his techniques and the histories of his Bibles continues. But at the same time the idea of 'Gutenberg' in popular imagination has drifted into a strangely ahistorical role in which the printer now serves more or less as the poster boy for the dawn of modernity, whose updated function is to embody the 'old school' media revolution that inspired and led to our own. Common knowledge of Gutenberg's 'immeasurable' importance often replaces facts. On 14 April 2021 bearded old Gutenberg was the funny face of the daily Google Doodle; easily accessible to 5 billion Internet users worldwide, the icon linked to a three-hundred-word puff piece in English called 'Celebrating Johannes Gutenberg', which generalized upon the global impact of his invention while failing to mention Asian printing and propagating at least a dozen basic factual errors. All too fittingly, in 2024, the first punchline in Broadway's *Gutenberg! The Musical!* (billed as 'highly inaccurate') established the half-jesting premise that since the facts concerning the world's most important invention were so scarce, further historical research was unnecessary.

Six centuries and more removed from his birth, the printer of the world's most expensive and most scrutinized book could hardly have been much more famous, and the appreciation of his contribution to humanity, at least among Western insiders, could hardly have been much greater. One might have asked, what about this 'Man of the Millennium', if anything, was left to rescue? Accepting that the plaques on his various monuments should not convey immoderate praise, overreaching claims or culturally biased misinformation, all that needs to be rescued, perhaps, is the *true* Gutenberg. If he were allowed to climb down from his unwanted public pedestal, the world might gain a better understanding of his true place in a more capacious and accurate global history. There is no denying that Gutenberg stood at the forefront of important changes in Western culture over the past half-millennium, but sadly his significance beyond Europe continues to be overstated, a circumstance that has made him a target for resentment and dismissal. Historians of early Asian book production grow weary of reading about Gutenberg's 'invention of printing' (defined no further), and in 2022 Kristina Richardson, a scholar of Middle Eastern and South Asian languages and cultures, voiced this far-reaching complaint:

> Print history is a deeply political field, as the supremacy of Western modernity rests almost entirely on representing print's origins as uniquely Christian and European and its effects on Latin Christendom as singularly transformative . . . The master narrative in studies of print culture claims that Johann Gutenberg, born into an aristocratic family around the year 1400, independently developed the printing press, *ex nihilo*, in Mainz, Germany, in a burst of inspired genius . . . The purity of Gutenberg's inspiration functions as a hagiography in service to a larger mythology, in this case the origin myth of European modernity as an endogenous development.[16]

Such a politicized master narrative certainly does exist, either by design or by default. While it is not supported by all of Gutenberg's admirers, neither is it consciously avoided by all. Almost inevitably, it seems, the historical facts are not handled responsibly, and the telling of associated myths only makes it worse. Hagiography has little historical or educational value, and it can do harm. Therefore, facts bear repetition, and the old assumptions and assertions invite thorough scrutiny and reconsideration.

Progenitors may be best understood by where their influence finally stops. Gutenberg's personal agency in the history of printing ended in 1468 at the latest. Once he had made his invention he was largely powerless to determine its fate. Of course his work had made that of subsequent printers possible, but for how many generations after his death did his invention remain strictly his invention? At what point did Gutenberg's own butterfly effect fade to a mere ripple within the torrent of ongoing histories? Much of the world never printed the way he taught his immediate followers to print and ever less and less of it relies on printing in order to make its global communications possible. Gutenberg's invention simply isn't doing that much for people anymore.

Is printing inherently good? Mark Twain reminded the founders of the Gutenberg Museum that it wasn't. Countless times printing had served the causes of freedom, learning and social good, and yet the 'Man of the Millennium' also used his press to broadcast religious intolerance and peddle worthless indulgences to underwrite sectarian warfare. Later, the repeatedly printed *Malleus maleficarum* (Hammer of Witches) drove fifteenth-century superstition, fear and misogyny; the Declaration of Independence, printed in the city of brotherly love on America's birthday in 1776, demonized 'the merciless Indian savages'; horrific affronts to humanity rolled from the printing presses in Nazi Germany and in response to the civil rights movement in the United States. Were these not also the responsibility of the 'Man of the Millennium'? To glorify the Western printing tradition unreservedly, remembering only its triumphs of social justice, scientific discovery and literary achievement, is not a valid view of history.

Bold assertions to the contrary, it is all too possible 'to overstate the significance of Johannes Gutenberg's development of moveable metal type', thereby exaggerating his impact upon modernity while misrepresenting the roles of other cultures and traditions. Consider this: if we had inherited only what Gutenberg himself invented, then the book now in your hands would be unwieldy and prohibitively expensive, severely limited in its availability, entirely unillustrated and unfamiliar in its lettering, lacking in notes (and parentheses), and you would still be filling in all of the necessary rubrication. The evolution of the typographic book was the work of countless hands, most of them unknown to the inventor. Moreover, Europe's first printer by no means provided millions of books for all levels of society throughout the world, nor was that achieved overnight. At Gutenberg's death, printing presses were still functioning in only six or seven towns. Averaging perhaps three hundred copies per edition, printed books were relatively few and far between, scattered across barely one-quarter of Europe – seen another way, the footprint of Gutenberg's initial influence overlay less than 2 per cent of the world's landmass, an area roughly the size of Algeria. Even so, his work and the vast majority of printing that followed was intended only for literate, affluent Christians and their wealthy religious institutions (printing by and for Jews did not emerge until after his death). Finally, to argue that moveable metal type printing made European books inherently more successful or progressive is to ignore the Korean achievements of the 1370s and to misrepresent much earlier Chinese book culture, which had achieved far greater volume and geographic reach, with no deficit of usefulness or sophistication. These perspectives should not render fifteenth-century European printing any less interesting, but they do reveal that Gutenberg's direct impact was far less 'global' or 'universal' than virtually every writer on the subject has admitted.

There can be no final assessment of Gutenberg's contributions: Fortune's wheel will continue to turn, and our picture of the man will continue to evolve as the coming generations reconsider his work and impact, be it for good or for evil. For now it will be better, and much less of a stretch, if we accept a downsized Gutenberg in our rhetoric and in our classrooms. If medieval Europe reaped what Gutenberg sowed and grew into something new and different, then that is legacy enough for a man of those times. Rescued from his precarious pedestal, Gutenberg emerges not as an oversized, 'fakey' statue that strives to embody an impossible claim, but as a man of flesh and blood, whose real-life ambitions, long-lost experiments, shared triumphs and vexing setbacks make his elusive old books all the more alive with historical interest. As the material reflections of a singular medieval life well spent, his books make a monument more lasting than bronze.

CHRONOLOGY

1400?   Johann Gensfleisch (zum Gutenberg) is born to a patrician
        family in Mainz
1428   During civil unrest Mainz expels its patrician families,
        including Gutenberg's, until 1430
1434   Residing in Strasbourg, Gutenberg is the defendant in a
        local defamation lawsuit
1436   Gutenberg is working in partnership with goldsmiths and
        stone-polishers in Strasbourg
1438   Gutenberg is manufacturing small mirrors in Strasbourg for
        sale to pilgrims at Aachen
1439   In a lawsuit against Gutenberg, the brothers of the late
        Andreas Dritzehn, stone-polisher, attempt to assume their
        brother's stake in a joint business venture in Strasbourg
1442   Gutenberg takes a loan from the Chapter of St Thomas in
        Strasbourg; he and Martin Brechter pay interest on it until
        1458
1444   Gutenberg pays Strasbourg taxes and registers for
        militia duty; these are the final documentary records of
        Gutenberg's residence in that city
1448   Living once again in Mainz, Gutenberg takes out a loan
        from Arnold Gelthus
1450   Large loans and investments provided by Johann Fust
        begin to finance Gutenberg's 'work of the books' in Mainz.
        This is a date that several early chroniclers associated with
        Gutenberg's invention of typography
1452   Approximate date of the fragmentary Sibyllenbuch, found
        in Mainz, believed to be the earliest surviving European
        printing with moveable types
1453   Constantinople falls to Sultan Mehmed II. Pope Nicholas V
        calls for a crusade against the Ottoman Empire
1454   Printed Cyprus indulgences are issued widely from Mainz
        between October 1454 and the following April; in October,
        a man selling many unfinished Bibles catches the attention
        of dignitaries at the Diet of Frankfurt; in December, the

	printed *Turkenkalender* warns Europe's leaders that they must confront Ottoman expansion in the New Year
1455	In March, Aeneas Silvius Piccolomini clarifies that the 'miraculous man' encountered at Frankfurt the previous autumn was selling quires from 158 to 180 copies of a handsome Bible (a copy of the 42-line Bible, Europe's earliest substantial typographic book, was rubricated throughout by August 1456). On 6 November 1455, seeking restitution of his loans and interest, Fust litigates the end of his partnership with Gutenberg concerning the 'work of the books'
1456	Latin and German editions of the *Bulla turcorum* of Callixtus III are printed in Mainz
1457	Fust and Peter Schoeffer publish the Mainz *Psalter*, Europe's first dated printed book. Gutenberg is a member of the lay-confraternity of St Viktor outside the walls of Mainz
1458	According to a lost document, Charles VII sends Nicolas Jenson, master of the Tours mint, to learn the art of printing from its 'inventor' in Mainz (identified as Gutenberg in some transcriptions)
1459	Diether von Isenburg is elected Archbishop of Mainz
1460	The *Catholicon*, a Latin dictionary by Giovanni Balbi, is printed anonymously in Mainz. A copy of Johann Mentelin's 49-line Latin Bible, printed in Strasbourg, is rubricated
1461	Date of rubrication found in a 36-line Bible, printed in Bamberg with Mainz types; in February, Albrecht Pfister begins to print books in Bamberg with these same types. Indulgences for rebuilding the church of St Cyriacus at Neuhausen are printed in Mainz
1462	Printers in Mainz publish broadsides regarding the contested archiepiscopacy of Mainz. On 28 October forces loyal to the papal appointee Adolph II von Nassau capture and sack the city. In retribution for the fierce local resistance, Adolph orders the exile of the male citizens of Mainz; Gutenberg probably decamps to nearby Eltville
1463	Printing in Mainz resumes with the publication of Pius II, *Bulla cruciata contra Turcos*
1464	The printer of the Mainz *Catholicon* publishes an indulgence for the Trinitarian Order

1465   Adolph II von Nassau, Archbishop of Mainz, rewards
Gutenberg with a generous pension for his 'agreeable
and voluntary service', making him a courtier within his
entourage

1466   Johann Fust dies in Paris; Peter Schoeffer continues to
print books in Mainz until 1502

1467   The Bechtermünze brothers commence printing in Eltville
with the *Catholicon* types

1468   Gutenberg dies in Mainz sometime before 26 February,
leaving 'numerous formes, letters, instruments, tools, and
other items pertaining to the work of printing' to another
investor, Dr Conrad Humery. Memorials of the invention
of printing begin to appear

REFERENCES

1 An Invention for Europe

1 Stanley J. Baran, *Introduction to Mass Communication, Media Literacy and Culture*, 8th edn (New York, 2014), p. 19.
2 Mark Twain, letter of 7 April 1900 to the German industrialist Adolf Goerz regarding the opening of the Gutenberg Museum in Mainz, published in *Gutenberg-Fest zu Mainz im Jahre 1900: Zugleich Erinnerungs-Gab an die Eröffnung des Gutenberg-Museums am 23. Juni 1901* (Mainz, 1901), pp. 13–14.
3 'Scema tabernaculi moises salomonque templi
  Haut preter ingenuos perficiunt dedalos,
  Sic decus ecclesie maius maior salomone
  Iam renovans, renovat beselehel et hyram.
  Hos dedit exemios sculpendi in arte magistros,
  Cui placet en mactos arte sagire viros.
  Quos genuit ambos urbs maguntina Johanne
  Librorum insignes prothocaragmaticos
  Cum quibus optatum Petrus venit ad poliandrum
  Cursu posterior introeundo prior.
  Quippe quibus praestat sculpendi lege sagitus
  A solo dante lumen et ingenium.'

  The difficult final word in verse 8, 'prothocaragmaticos', derives from the Greek root for 'character', *caragma* (a stamping tool), which the Mainz *Catholicon* of 1460 defined as an 'impression, image, or letter', quoting Anianus (that is, Pseudo-Chrysostom, *Opus imperfectum in Mattheum*, Homily 38): *Sicut numus habet charagma Caesaris, sic habet homo charagma Dei* ('As a coin bears the stamp of Caesar, so a man bears the stamp of God').
4 Johannes Trithemius, *Annales Hirsaugienses* (St Gall, 1690), vol. II, ff. 421–2, under the year 1450: 'His temporibus in civitate Moguntina Germaniae prope Rhenum, et non in Italia, ut quidam falso scripserunt, inventa et excogitata est ars illa mirabilis et prius inaudita imprimendi et characterizandi libros per Joannem Guttenberger, civem Moguntinum.'

5 Fichet's letter was published in Gasparinus Barzizius, *Orthographia* (Paris: Ulrich Gering, Martin Crantz and Michael Friburger, after 1 January 1471), ff. 1v–2r: 'De studiorum humanitatis restitutione loquor. Quibus (quantum ipse coniectura capio) magnum lumen novorum librariorum genus attulit, quos nostra memoria (sicut quidam equus troianus) quoquo versus effudit germania. Ferunt enim illic, haut procul a civitate Maguncia, Ioannem quendam fuisse, cui cognomen bonemontano, qui primus omnium impressoriam artem excogitaverit, qua non calamo (ut prisci quidem illi) neque penna (ut nos fingimus) sed aereis litteris libri finguntur, et quidem expedite, polite, et pulchre.'

6 Martin Davies, '"Non ve n'è ignuno a stampa": The Printed Books of Federico da Montefeltro', in *Federico da Montefeltro and his Library*, ed. Marcello Simonetta (Milan, 2007), pp. 63–78.

7 Folio 1v: 'Accedebant justae preces magistri Nicolai Jenson Gallici alterius (ut vere dicam) Daedali: qui librariae artis mirabilis inventor: non ut scribantur calamo libri: sed veluti gemma imprimantur: ac prope sigillo primus omnium ingeniose monstravit.'

8 The passage on printing appears on ff. 121r–v: 'Jacobus cognominato Gutenbergo: patria Argentinus & quidam alter cui nomen Fustus imprimendarum litterarum in membranis cum metallicis formis periti trecentas cartas quisque eorum per diem facere innotescunt apud Maguntiam Germaniae civitatem. Iohannes quoque, Mentelinus nuncupatus, apud Argentinam eiusdem provinciae civitatem, ac in eodem artificio peritus, totidem cartas per diem imprimere agnoscitur.'

9 'Quantum litterarum studiosi Germanis debeant nullo satis dicendi genere exprimi posset. Namque a Joanne Gutenberg Zumiungen equiti Maguntiae rheni solerti ingenio librorum Imprimendorum ratio 1440. inventa: hoc tempore in omnes fere orbis partes propagantur: quam omnis antiquitas parvo aerae comparata: posterioribus infinitis voluminibus legitur.'

10 Johannes Trithemius, *Opera historica*, ed. Marquard Freher, vol. II (Frankfurt am Main: Heirs of Andreas Wechel, for Claude de Marne, 1601), p. 556, letter 44 (6 August 1507): 'Ars enim quam impressoriam vocant tempore infantiae meae apud Moguntiam metropolim Francorum inventa, infinita pene et veterum et novorum volumina quotidie producit in lucem.'

11 Florence, Biblioteca Medicea Laurenziana, Conv. Soppr. 133, f. 82r: '1449: Maguntie in Germania Robertus Dusberch novo invento

claret, quo libros supra trecentos eo temporis spatio imprimerit quo vix singuli calamo perscriberentur.'

12 Folio cccxii [gg2] recto: 'Item dese hoichwyrdige kunst vursz is vonden aller eyrst in Duytschlant tzo Mentz am Rijne. Ind dat is der duytsch'scher nacion eyn groisse eirlicheit dat sulche synriiche mynschen syn dae tzo vynden. Ind dat is geschiet by den iairen uns heren anno domini mccccxl. Ind van der zijt an bis men schreve L. [50] wart undersoicht die kunst ind wat dair zo gehoirt. Ind in den iairen uns heren do men schreyff mccccl. do was eyn gulden iair, do began men tzo drucken ind was dat eyrste boich dat men druckde die Bybel zo latijn, ind wart gedruckt mit eynre grover schrifft. as is die schrifft dae men nu Mysseboicher mit druckt.'

13 'Mer der eyrste vynder der druckerye is gewest eyn Burger tzo Mentz. ind was geboren van Straiszburch. ind heisch joncker Johan Gudenburch.'

2 A Man Called Gutenberg

1 Aeneas Silvius Piccolomini, *De ritu, situ, moribus et conditione Teutoniae, sive Germania* (Leipzig: Wolfgang Stöckel, 9 April 1496), f. 18r: 'Maguntia, urbs vetusta, Variana clade insignis, templorum magnificentia et privatis ac publicis edificiis exornata, nihil habet, quod reprehendere queas nisi vicorum artitudinem.'

2 'Messire Guthemberg Chevalier demeurant a Mayence . . . avoit mis en lumière l'invention d'imprimer.' Gutenberg's name is not included in all of the early transcriptions; see Lotte Hellinga, 'Nicolas Jenson, Peter Schoeffer and the Development of Printing Types', in Lotte Hellinga, *Incunabula in Transit: People and Trade* (Leiden, 2018), pp. 40–88 (p. 56).

3 Kurt Köster, *Gutenberg in Strassburg* (Mainz, 1973), p. 11: 'in die Ochefart zu den spiegeln'.

3 In Golden Mainz

1 The author is grateful to Dr Sara Poor of Princeton University for her advice regarding this translation.

2 Paris, Bibliothèque nationale, Rés. vél. 1038: 'Explicit donatus. Arte nova imprimendi seu caracterizandi per Petrum de gernszheym in urbe Moguntina cum suis capitalibus absque calami exaratione effigiatus.'

3 'In dem selbin jare quam abir ein legate von Rome gein Erffurtte und wiszete grosze bollen von unsirme heiligen vater, dem bobiste

Nicolao dem funfften, in haldene grosze gnade. Der selbe legate gab brive von sich den jhenen, die des aplas gebruchten, und er sammete groz gelt in der stad und uf dem lande.' See Falk Eisermann, 'The Indulgence as a Media Event: Developments in Communication through Broadsides in the Fifteenth Century', in *Promissory Notes on the Treasury of Merits: Indulgences in Late Medieval Europe*, ed. Robert N. Swanson (Leiden, 2006), pp. 309–30 (p. 311).

4 Kai-Michael Sprenger, '"Volumus tamen, quod expressio fiat ante finem mensis Maii presentis". Sollte Gutenberg 1452 im Auftrag Nikolaus von Kues' Ablaßbriefe drucken?', *Gutenberg-Jahrbuch*, LXXIV (1999), pp. 42–57.

4 The Work of the Books

1 The present translation is based on Martin Davies, 'Juan de Carvajal and Early Printing: The 42-Line Bible and the Sweynheym and Pannartz Aquinas', *The Library*, 6th series, XVIII/3 (September 1996), p. 196.

2 The letter was printed in Pius II [Aeneas Sylvius Piccolomini], *Epistolae saeculares et pontificales* (Cologne: Arnold Therhoernen, c. 1480); f. 120v.

3 John Jefferson, 'Rudolph von Rüdesheim: ein Zeitgenosse Gutenbergs', in *Reviewing Gutenberg: Historische Konzepte und Rezeptionen* (Stuttgart, 2021), ed. Michael Matheus, Heidrun Ochs and Kai-Michael Sprenger, pp. 163–4.

4 Richard Schwab et al., 'New Evidence on the Printing of the Gutenberg Bible: The Inks in the Doheny Copy', *Papers of the Bibliographical Society of America*, LXXVII/3 (1985), pp. 375–410; 'Ink Patterns in the Gutenberg New Testament: The Proton Milliprobe Analysis of the Lilly Library Copy', *PBSA*, LXXX/3 (1986), pp. 305–31; 'The Proton Milliprobe Ink Analysis of the Harvard B42, Volume II', *PBSA*, LXXXI/4 (1987), pp. 403–32.

5 'Iste liber illuminatus ligatus et completus est per henricum Cremer vicarium ecclesie collegate sancti Stephani Maguntinis sub anno domini Millesimo quadrigentesimo quinquagesimo sexto festo Assumpcionis gloriose virginis Marie Deo gracias Alleluia.'

6 'Et sic est finis prime partis biblie scilicet veteris testamenti illuminata seu rubricata et ligata per henricum Albch alias Cremer Anno domini Mcccclvi festo Bartholomei apostoli. Deo gratias. Alleluia.'

7 Hans-Michael Empell, *Gutenberg vor Gericht. Der Mainzer Prozess um die erste gedruckte Bibel* (Frankfurt am Main, 2008).

5 The Wonderful Concord

1 The only recorded copy was last seen in Kiev in 1937; see Boris Ivanovich Zdanevich, *Provinciale Romanum: Unbekannter Druck von Johannes Gutenberg* (Kiev, 1941).

2 For the text in translation, see James D. Mixson, *The Crusade of 1456: Texts and Documentation in Translation* (Toronto, 2022).

3 Paris, Bibliothèque nationale, Rés. v. 725. Only the upper half of the text survives: January through June and the first line of July.

4 The unique broadside is Munich, Universitätsbibliothek, Cim. 96; the manuscript is Mainz, Stadtbibliothek, Hs 1 290.

5 Carl Wehmer, *Mainzer Probedrucke in des Type der sogenannten astronomischen Kalenders für 1448* (Munich, 1948).

6 *Psalterium* ([Mainz], 1457), f. 143v (or 175v): 'Presens spalmorum codex, venustate capitalium decoratus Rubricationibusque sufficienter distinctus, Adinventione artificiosa imprimendi ac caracterizandi, absque calami ulla exaracione sic effigiatus, Et ad eusebiam dei industrie est consummatus, per Iohannem fust Civem maguntinum, Et Petrum Schoffer de Gernszheim. Anno domini millesimo. cccc. lvij. In vigilia Assumpcionis.'

7 Keffer's donation is recorded in Paris, Bibliothèque nationale, Rés. D. 7225: 'Hos duos sexternos accomidavit mihi heynricus Keppfer de moguncia nunquam revenit ut reacciperetur.'

8 The manuscript of 1458, richly illuminated by Heinrich Molitor and long owned by the Augustinians of the Holy Cross in Augsburg, is at Princeton University's Scheide Library (M163); the second, completed in 1462 for the Cistercians of Aldersbach, near Passau, is in Munich's Bavarian State Library (Clm 2795).

6 A Trojan Horse

1 Karl Hegel, ed., *Die Chroniken der deutschen Städte vom 14. bis ins 16. Jahrhunderts 18: Die Chroniken der mittelrheinischen Städte. Mainz*, part 2 (Leipzig, 1881), pp. 10–11 (introduction) and 45 (text), lines 12–16: 'undt wurden viel Exemplar getrukt von dem ersten Buchtrucker zu Meincz Johann Guttenbergk'.

2 'Wir Adolff . . . bekennen . . . das wir haben aangesehenn annemige und willige dinst, die uns und unsserm stifft unser lieber getruwer

Johann Gudenberg gethain hait . . . dar umb . . . ine zu unnserm
dhiener unnd hoifgesinde uffgnommen . . . Wir sullen unnd wollen
ime auch solichen dinst dwile er lebet, nit uffsagen, und uff dass er
solichs dinstes destabas gewesen moge, so wollen wir ine alle iar
. . . wan wir unnser gemeynnhoiffgesinde kleyden werden . . . glich
unnssern edeln kleyden unnd unser hoifkleydung geben laissen,
unnd alle iar eyns iglichen iars zwenczigmalder korns und zweii
fuder wins zu gebruchung sines hußs – doch das er die nit verkeuffe
ader verschengke, frii ane ungelt, nydderlage unnd wegegelt inn
unser stait Mentze iingeen laissen, ine auch, dwile er lebt unnd
unnser dhiener sine unnd bliben wirdet, wachens, vollge dynste,
schatzunge unnd anderer . . . gnediglich erlaissen. Unnd hait uns
daruber der egenant Johann Gudenberg in truwen globt . . . zu
Eltvil am donrstag sant Antonii tag [1465].' See Aloys Ruppel,
Johannes Gutenberg: Sein Leben und Werk (Nieuwkoop, 1967),
pp. 56–7.

3 'In foelicem artis impressorie inventorem/ D[eo] O[ptimo] M[aximo]
S[acrum]/ Ioanni Genszfleisch artis impressorie repertori de omni/
natione & lingua optime merito in nominis sui memoriam imor-/
talem. Adam Gelthus posuit ossa eius in ecclesia divi Francisci/
Maguntina foeliciter cubant.'

4 'Foelix Ansicare per te germania foelix/ Omnibus in terris premia
laudis habet./ Urbe Moguntina divino fulte Joannes/ Ingenio:
primus imprimis ere notas./ Multum relligio, multum tibi greca
sophia/ Et multum debet lingua latina tibi.'

7 Gutenberg's Rescue

1 'In welicher stadt auch anfengklich die wunderbare kunst der
Trückerey, und im ersten von dem kunstreichen Johan Güttenbergk
do mann zalt nach Christi nach Christi unsers heren gebürth
Tausent vierhunderth und fünffzig Jare erfunden, von und darnach
mit vleyss kost und arbeyt Johan Fausten und Peter Schöffers zu
Mentz gebesserth.'

2 The key passage reads: 'Anno autem MCCCCLII perfecit deduxitque
eam (divina favente gratia) in opus imprimendi (opera tamen ac
multis necessariis adinventionibus PETRI Schöffer de Gernsheim
ministri suiquem filii adoptivi) . . .'

3 See vol. III, p. 624: 'Addo typographicam & bombardariam, generi
humano utilissimas artes, quarum inventio Germanorum est.
C[astulus answers]: De istis duobus inventis audire perlubet, narra

obsecro. G[odefridus]: Anno à puerpera Virgine 1440. Friderico III. Imp. Ioannes Gutenbergius equestri nobilitate vir, Moguntiae rationem aeneis typis scribendi excogitavit. Quae à parvis ducta initiis, eo crevit humani ingenii sollertia, ut ad summam perfectionem brevi tempore accesserit. Divinum utique & admiratione dignissimum inventum. Vix enim credi potest, uno die, unum hominem tantum formare litterarum, quantum vel celerrimus scriba duobus annis vix possit.'

4 Niedersächsisches Landesarchiv Wolfenbüttel, 1 Alt 22 no. 83, f. 26r: 'Biblia latina, pars prima et secunda, vff Pergamein gedruckt In dem aller ersten vnd eltesten gedruck, Da die Druckerey erst angefangen In folio vnd in bretern mit gelem semischen leder vbertzogen, vnd mit meßings Puckeln vnd Clausuren beschlagen gebunden.'

5 'D. 44. Biblia latina vulgata, V. et N.T. per Jo. Faust impressa, (Mogunt. 1460) Voll. ii. Editio prima, splendidissima, rarissima et in Membrana impressa, c. literis initialibus variis coloribus pictis et Deauratis.'

6 'Anmerkungen von der alleraltesten und ersten gedruckten Ausgabe der Lateinischen Bibel, welche in der hiesigen Königlichen Bibliothek angetroffen wird', *Berlinische Bibliothek*, 1/2 (1747), pp. 269–82.

7 Samuel Engel, 'IIIme Lettre sur l'Origine de l'Imprimerie servant de Réponse à celle de Mr. Baulacre, célèbre Bibliothécaire, de Genève,' *Journal helvétique, ou Recueil de pièces fugitives de littérature choisie* (September 1745), pp. 195–220.

8 Martin Gerbert, *Iter Alemannicum accedit Italicum et Gallicum* (Sankt Blasien, 1765), pp. 157–64; Gerard Meerman, *Conspectus originum typographicarum* (The Hague, 1761), pp. 44–6 (notes).

9 Jean-Baptiste Maugerard, *Extrait du Mémoire lu à la séance du 24 Août 1789 de la Société royale des sciences et des arts de Metz par Dom Maugerard, bibliothécaire de M. le cardinal de Montmorency et de l'Abbaye S. Arnould, sur la découverte d'un exemplaire de la Bible connue sous le nom de Guttemberg, accompagné de renseignements, qui prouvent que l'impression de cette Bible est antérieure à celle du Psautier de 1457. Signé par Dupré de Genest* (Metz, 1789).

10 Cloots championed 'la Mémoire du premier révolutionnaire, du premier bienfaiteur des humains'. *Archives parlementaires de 1787 à 1860: recueil complet des débats législatifs et politiques des chambres françaises. Première série (1787 à 1799)*, XLIX (Paris, 1896), pp. 498–501.

11 Georg Christian Gottlieb Wedekind, 'Das Lob der
   Buchdruckerkunst. Ein Vorschlag an die Mainzer. Cloots Rede',
   in *Der Patriot* (Mainz, 1792), pp. 1–21.

12 *Gedenkbuch an die festlichen Tage der Inauguration des Gutenberg-
   Denkmals zu Mainz* (Mainz, 1837).

13 Pierre Henri Requin, 'Documents inédits sur les origines de
   la typographie', *Bulletin historique et philologique* (Paris, 1890),
   p. 9, doc. 1: 'duo abecedaria calibis et duas formas ferreas, unum
   instrumentum calibis vocatum vitis, quadraginta octo formas
   stangni necnon diversas alias formas ad artem scribendi pertinentes'.

14 Allan Stevenson, *The Problem of the Missale Speciale* (London,
   1967).

15 Blaise Agüera y Arcas, 'Temporary Matrices and Elemental
   Punches in Gutenberg's DK Type', in *Incunabula and Their Readers:
   Printing, Selling and Using Books in the Fifteenth Century*, ed. Kristian
   Jensen (London, 2003), pp. 1–12, incorporating research by Paul
   Needham.

16 Kristina Richardson, *Roma in the Medieval Islamic World: Literacy,
   Culture, and Migration* (London, 2022), pp. 103–4.

RECOMMENDED READING

The most complete biography of Johann Gutenberg is Guy Bechtel, *Gutenberg et l'invention de l'imprimerie. Une enquête* (Paris, 1992). English readers may prefer Sabina Wagner's chapter 'A Well-Known Stranger', translated from German in *Gutenberg: Man of the Millennium* (Mainz, 2000), pp. 114–39; Albert Kapr's *Johann Gutenberg: The Man and his Invention*, trans. Douglas Martin (Aldershot, 1996) is less reliable. Douglas McMurtrie's *The Gutenberg Documents* (New York, 1941) summarizes the essential documentary work of Karl Schorbach, published in Germany in 1900. Hans-Michael Empell, *Gutenberg vor Gericht. Der Mainzer Prozess um die erste gedruckte Bibel* (Frankfurt am Main, 2008) presents the most reliable interpretation of the Helmasperger Instrument.

Earlier printing traditions are usefully treated in James Soren Edgren, 'The History of the Book in China', in *The Oxford Companion to the Book*, 2 vols, ed. Michael F. Suarez and H. R. Woudhuysen (Oxford, 2010), vol. I, pp. 353–65, and Kristina Richardson, *Roma in the Medieval Islamic World: Literacy, Culture, and Migration* (London, 2022), pp. 103–38. For background on Gutenberg's work in Strasbourg, see Otto Fuhrmann, *Gutenberg and the Strasbourg Documents of 1439* (New York, 1940). Context for Gutenberg's production of pilgrims' mirrors is found in Ann Marie Rasmussen, *Medieval Badges: Their Wearers and Their Worlds* (Philadelphia, PA, 2021).

A useful checklist of European printed editions during Gutenberg's time is found in Margaret Bingham Stillwell, *The Beginning of the World of Books, 1450 to 1470: A Chronological Survey of the Texts Chosen for Printing during the First Twenty Years of the Printing Art. With a Synopsis of the Gutenberg Documents* (New York, 1972). For blockbooks, see Nigel F. Palmer, 'Blockbooks: Texts and Illustrations Printed from Wood Blocks', *Journal of the Printing History Society*, 11 (Spring 2008), pp. 5–23.

For the Gutenberg Bible, see Janet Ing's slender but excellent *Johann Gutenberg and His Bible: A Historical Study* (New York, 1988), and for the stories of each copy, see Eric Marshall White, *Editio princeps: A History of the Gutenberg Bible* (Turnhout, 2017). The indispensible analysis of the Bible's production is Paul Needham, 'The Paper Supply of the Gutenberg Bible', *Papers of the Bibliographical Society of America*, LXXIX/3 (1985), pp. 303–74.

The essential source for the Mainz *Catholicon* of 1460 is Paul Needham, 'Johann Gutenberg and the Catholicon Press', *Papers of the Bibliographical Society of America*, LXXVI/4 (1982), pp. 395–456. Also of relevance to printing in Mainz are Irvine Masson, *The Mainz Psalters and Canon Missae, 1457–1459* (London, 1954), and Hellmut Lehmann-Haupt's *Peter Schoeffer of Gernsheim and Mainz* (Rochester, NY, 1950). Two broader views of Gutenberg's legacy are Stephan Füssel's *Gutenberg and the Impact of Printing*, trans. Douglas Martin (Aldershot, 2003), and Frédéric Barbier's *Gutenberg's Europe: The Book and the Invention of Western Modernity* (Cambridge, 2017).

ACKNOWLEDGEMENTS

I first became deeply interested in Gutenberg's work in 1997, when I was hired as curator of rare books at Southern Methodist University's Bridwell Library in Dallas, which happened to own interesting fragments of three different Gutenberg Bibles. My first book, *Editio princeps: A History of the Gutenberg Bible*, published in 2017, told the often forgotten backstories of each of the 48 surviving Bibles (and numerous fragments) since their rediscovery, but it necessarily relegated Gutenberg himself, and many other fascinating aspects of his career, to the background. The present biography of Gutenberg is the result of many years of thinking about this even more elusive topic. My work would not have been possible without the cumulative input (over countless coffees) of Dr Paul Needham, Scheide Librarian Emeritus at Princeton University, and (over countless meals and nature walks) my wife, Dr Pamela Patton, Director of the Index of Medieval Art at Princeton University. Each of them in their own ways helped me see Gutenberg and his real place in the world more clearly.

PHOTO ACKNOWLEDGEMENTS

The author and publishers wish to express their thanks to the sources listed below for illustrative material and/or permission to reproduce it:

akg-images: 34; © S. Ballard 2024: 3; Bayerische Staatsbibliothek, Munich, photos World Digital Library: 11, 23; Bridwell Library, Perkins School of Theology, Southern Methodist University, Dallas, TX: 41; Cambridge University Library (Inc.0.A.1.2[6]): 31; collection of the author: 1; collection Van Beuningen Family, Netherlands: 14; Cotsen Children's Library, Princeton University, NJ: 48; from *Die Cronica van der hilliger stat van Coellen* (Cologne: Johann Koelhoff II, 23 August 1499), photo Princeton University Library, NJ: 8; from Karl Dziatzko, *Gutenbergs früheste Druckerpraxis* (Berlin, 1890), photo Princeton University Library, NJ: 57; from Eusebius of Caesarea, *Chronicon* (Venice: Erhard Ratdolt, 1483), photo Princeton University Library, NJ: 7; Generallandesarchiv Karlsruhe (67 Nr. 1057, fol. 277v): 13; Gutenberg-Museum, Mainz: 16; Handschriftenabteilung, Staatsbibliothek zu Berlin (Inv.-Nr. Portr. Slg/Slg Wadzeck/Bd. 30/Nr. 233): 54; from Leonhard Hoffmann, 'Ist Gutenberg der Drucker des Catholicon?', *Zentralblatt für Bibliothekswesen*, XCIII (Leipzig, 1979), photo Princeton University Library, NJ: 44; The Huntington Library, San Marino, CA (RB 92588): 24; John Rylands Research Institute and Library, University of Manchester: 6 (Blockbook 3103), 22 (17250.2), 25 (Spencer 3069), 45 (Incunable 9375), 50 (313); Kupferstichkabinett, Staatliche Museen zu Berlin (Inv.-Nr. KdZ 30697), photo Dietmar Katz: 10; photo lapping/Pixabay: 12; Library of Congress, Rare Book and Special Collections Division, Washington, DC (Lessing J. Rosenwald Collection): 26; The Morgan Library & Museum, New York (PML 12, fol. 5r): 29; courtesy Paul Needham: 53; Real Academia de la Historia, Madrid: 42; Scheide Library, Princeton University, NJ: 2 (photo Shelley Szwast), 4, 5, 17, 19, 21, 27, 28, 33, 35, 36, 37, 38, 39, 40, 46, 47, 49, 51, 52; from Johann Daniel Schöpflin, *Vindiciae typographicae* (Strasbourg: Johann Gottfried Bauer, 1760), photo Zentralbibliothek Zurich: 20; Staatsarchiv Ludwigsburg (B 389 Bü 586): 43; Staatsarchiv Nürnberg (Inv.-Nr. Rst. N. Handschriften Nr. 399a): 15; from André Thévet, *Les vrais pourtraits et vies des hommes illustres* (Paris: Widow of Jacques Kerver and Guillaume Chaudrier, 1584), photo Princeton University Library, NJ: 9; Universitäts- und Landesbibliothek Darmstadt: 18; Universitätsbibliothek Würzburg (M.p.th.f.m.11-2, fol. 205r): 30; Wikimedia Commons: 55 (Gutenberg-Museum, Mainz; photo Martinvl, CC BY-SA 3.0 DE); photo Jan Zahle/Thorvaldsens Museum: 56; from Boris Ivanovich Zdanevich, *Provinciale Romanum: Unbekannter Druck von Johannes Gutenberg* (Kiev, 1941): 32.

INDEX

Illustration numbers are indicated by *italics*